BLACK & DECKER ®

THE COMPLETE GUIDE TO
CERAMIC & STONE TILE

*Techniques & Projects
with Ceramics, Natural Stone
& Mosaics*

CREATIVE
PUBLISHING
international

CHANHASSEN, MINNESOTA

www.creativepub.com

Contents

Basics

Copyright © 2003
Creative Publishing international, Inc.
18705 Lake Drive East
Chanhassen, Minnesota 55317
1-800-328-3895
www.creativepub.com
All rights reserved

Printed on American Paper by: R.R. Donnelley

10 9 8 7 6 5 4 3

President/CEO: Michael Eleftheriou
Vice President/Publisher: Linda Ball
Vice President/Retail Sales & Marketing: Kevin Haas

Executive Editor: Bryan Trandem
Creative Director: Tim Himsel
Editorial Director: Jerri Farris
Managing Editor: Michelle Skudlarek

Lead Editor: Jerri Farris
Editors: Nancy Baldrica, Andrew Karre, Karen Ruth
Art Director: Kari Johnston
Mac Designer: Jon Simpson
Project Manager: Tracy Stanley
Photo Researchers: Julie Caruso, Andrew Karre
Copy Editor: Janice Cauley
Technical Illustrator: Earl Slack
Studio Services Manager: Jeanette Moss McCurdy
Photo Team Leader: Tate Carlson
Photographers: Chuck Nields, Andrea Rugg
Scene Shop Carpenter: Randy Austin
Photo Stylists: Theresa Henn, Joanne Wawra
Director of Production Services & Photography: Kim Gerber
Production Manager: Stasia Dorn

Cover photo courtesy of Sicis Mosaic & Art®,
from the Country Floors® Signature Collection

THE COMPLETE GUIDE TO CERAMIC & STONE TILE
Created by: The Editors of Creative Publishing international, Inc.,
in cooperation with Black & Decker. Black & Decker is a trademark
of The Black & Decker Corporation and is used under license.

Projects

Library of Congress
Cataloging-in-Publication Data

The complete guide to ceramic & stone
tile : techniques & projects with ceramics,
natural stone & mosaics.
    p. cm.
    Includes index.
    ISBN 1-58923-094-9 (soft cover)
    1. Tile laying--Amateurs' manuals.
2. Tiles--Amateurs' manuals. I. Title: At
head of title: Black & Decker. II. Creative
Publishing International.

TH8531.C65 2003
698--dc21

          2003053266

Portions of *The Complete Guide to Ceramic &
Stone Tile* are taken from the Black & Decker®
books *Bathroom Remodeling; Remodeling
Kitchens; Flooring Projects & Techniques; Customizing Your Home.* Other titles from Creative
Publishing international include:

*The New Everyday Home Repairs; Basic Wiring
& Electrical Repairs; Building Decks; Home Masonry Projects & Repairs; Workshop Tips &
Techniques; Carpentry: Remodeling; Carpentry:
Tools • Shelves • Walls • Doors; Exterior Home
Repairs & Improvements; Home Plumbing
Projects & Repairs; Advanced Home Wiring;
Advanced Deck Building; Built-In Projects for
the Home; Landscape Design & Construction;
Refinishing & Finishing Wood; Building Porches
& Patios; Advanced Home Plumbing; Remodeling
Kitchens, Finishing Basements & Attics;
Stonework & Masonry Projects; Sheds, Gazebos
& Outbuildings; Building & Finishing Walls &
Ceilings; The Complete Guide to Home Plumbing;
The Complete Guide to Home Wiring; The Complete Guide to Building Decks; The Complete
Guide to Painting & Decorating; The Complete
Guide to Creative Landscapes; The Complete
Guide to Home Masonry; The Complete Guide to
Home Carpentry; The Complete Guide to Home
Storage; The Complete Guide to Windows &
Doors; The Complete Guide to Bathrooms; The
Complete Photo Guide to Home Repair; The
Complete Photo Guide to Home Improvement;
The Complete Photo Guide to Outdoor Home
Improvement.*

Introduction

Tile is a natural choice for your home. Literally a natural choice because whether it's ceramic, porcelain, natural stone, glass, or metal, virtually all tile begins with materials mined from the earth. And figuratively a natural choice because tile is attractive, durable, easy to maintain and (most often) affordable.

Before we get into the many reasons for tile's popularity, let's take a quick look at its history. The first tile made of fired-clay was produced before recorded history. That's right—*before recorded history*. Someone must have noticed that wet clay hardened when it dried. And someone else must have figured out that clay hardened even more when it was subjected to heat. It wasn't much of a leap from there to realize that higher temperatures produced harder tile.

Estimates vary regarding the first use of tile, but archaeologists have discovered a kiln near Sienna, Italy, believed to date from the 3rd century B.C. And some scientists believe that Egyptians used colored glazes on fired clay more than 6,000 years ago. What is not in dispute is that tile has been found in the pyramids as well as in the ruins of Babylon and of ancient Greek cities. And talk about durability: Intact tile has been found in the excavation of Pompeii. Pretty remarkable considering that it was buried in ash for most of the preceding 2,000 years.

By the Middle Ages, handmade tile graced the walls and floors of hundreds—if not thousands—of monasteries and other important buildings across the known world. By the 17th century, the production of tile was so important that

England developed strict manufacturing standards and exacted substantial penalties for violating them. By the 1800s, newer, more efficient manufacturing processes brought the price of tile within reason and it began to be used in homes as well as religious and public buildings.

Today, tile is used in homes and commercial buildings on every continent, probably because it makes sense in so many settings. What other material is so versatile? Tile can be smooth or rough, intricate or simple, colorful or muted. It provides excellent insulation properties, doesn't give off toxic fumes in a fire, withstands exposure to light, and repels moisture. In fact, tile rated as impervious is so easy to clean that it's often used on walls and floors in commercial food preparation areas and operating rooms.

In your home, tile can produce dozens of illusions, making rooms seem larger or more intimate, brighter or cozier, grandly formal or uniquely artistic. Although you may think of tile as primarily for entries, bathrooms, and kitchens, there's no reason to limit its use to those rooms. Living rooms, family rooms, bedrooms—as the photographs throughout this book attest, tile can beautify any room in your house. And with the help of *The Complete Guide to Ceramic & Stone Tile*, you can make it happen.

Starting with the removal of current floor and wall coverings and moving all the way through the planning process right into the final touches, we'll be with you all the way. We'll take a look at the types of tools and materials you'll need and guide you through the process of selecting tile for your projects. And when it comes time to implement your plans, you'll find plenty of clear photographs and thorough step-by-step instructions that can be adapted to your specific needs.

So, what are you waiting for? Let's get started.

Selecting Tile

Floor Tile

Floor tile needs to be more than just attractive—it needs to be strong and durable as well. After all, floors bear the weight of furniture and foot traffic, not to mention the sudden impact of every one and every thing that falls on them. Floor tile is engineered to tolerate these stresses.

Most floor tile also is suitable for countertops. And although it's generally thicker and heavier than wall tile, many styles of floor tile can be used on walls. The trim pieces necessary for counters and walls aren't always available, though, which may limit your options.

When shopping for tile, look for ratings by the American National Standards Institute or the Porcelain Enamel Institute (see page 13). If ratings aren't available, check with your dealer to make sure the tile you're considering is suitable for your project.

Before you start shopping, consider where the tile will be used and what you want it to accomplish. Will it be exposed to moisture? Should it be a focal point or a subtle background? Do you want it to establish the room's color palette or blend into it? The range of available options is truly mind-boggling—establishing some guidelines before you go shopping will simplify the selection process enormously. This section provides information that will help you select floor tile.

Photos this page courtesy of Crossville Porcelain Stone

Striking combinations of neutral colors (above) create shape and texture in this traditional sitting room.

Muted colors and a subtle design (left) provide an attractive background for the interesting architectural features and accessories of this entry.

A WORD ON RATINGS

Floor tile often comes labeled with water absorption and PEI (Porcelain Enamel Institute) ratings. Absorption is a concern because tile that soaks up water is susceptible to mildew and mold and can be difficult to clean. Ratings indicate how a tile can be used and whether or not it needs to be sealed against moisture. Tile is rated non-vitreous, semi-vitreous, vitreous, or impervious, in increasing order of water resistance. Non-vitreous tile is quite porous; semi-vitreous is used in dry-to-occasionally-wet locations; vitreous tile can be used without regard to its exposure to moisture. Impervious tile generally is reserved for restaurants, hospitals, and commercial applications where sanitation is a special concern.

The PEI number is a wear rating that indicates how the tile should be used. Ratings of 1 and 2 indicate tile is suitable for walls only; tile rated 3 and 4 is suitable for all residential applications—walls, counters, and floors. Most tile carries absorption and PEI ratings, but some—especially imported and art tiles—may not. Ask the retailer if you're not sure.

Depending on the retailer, tile may also have other ratings. Some tile is graded 1 to 3 for the quality of manufacturing. Grade 1 indicates standard grade; 2 indicates minor glaze and size flaws; 3 indicates major flaws; use for decoration only. Tile suitable for outdoor use is sometime rated with regard to its resistance to frost. Finally, coefficient of friction numbers may be included with some tile. The higher the coefficient, the more slip resistant the tile. A dry coefficient of .6 is the minimum standard for the Americans with Disabilities Act.

Glazed Ceramic Tile

Glazed ceramic tile is made from clay pressed into a shape by machine and then fired in a kiln. An amazing array of shapes, sizes, and thicknesses is possible. The critical part isn't the tile itself, but the glaze applied to the tile before firing. The glaze, made up of a number of glass and metal elements, provides color and creates a hard, shiny surface.

Glaze is supposed to be smooth and hard, but for floors, smooth and hard could also mean slick or slippery when wet. Most glazed ceramic tile for floors is designed to avoid those problems. The surface on some is textured or given a slightly raised design; on others the glaze itself includes materials added to create a non-skid surface.

Glazed tile generally absorbs very little or no water, making it both easy to maintain and mildew resistant. If the glaze is hard and scratch resistant and the tile properly installed and maintained, a glazed ceramic tile floor will last for decades.

Glazes sometimes include materials that create non-slip surfaces as well as a wide range of colors (above).

Simple tiles become sophisticated floors when contrasting colors are arranged in striking patterns (right).

Porcelain Tile

Porcelain tile is produced by pressing refined white clay into shape and then firing it in a kiln at very high temperatures. The resulting tile is extremely hard, absorbs very little or no water, and doesn't stain or mildew.

Porcelain tile is manufactured in all shapes and sizes, and, because its base color is white, there is virtually no limit to the colors and finishes available. Tile makers can also imprint textures when the tile is pressed, giving them slip-resistant surfaces well suited for wet locations.

Color is not added to porcelain tile with glaze (as it is with ceramic tile). Instead, dye is mixed into the clay and so goes all the way through the tile—a very good thing if you ever chip one. The lack of a glaze also means that tile makers can press finer, more intricate textures and patterns into the tile when it is manufactured. Porcelain tile can even be pressed so that it's nearly indistinguishable from cut stone, which tends to be more expensive but less durable. For ease of maintenance, porcelain is hard to beat. Its smooth finish and imperviousness to moisture keep soil and stains from setting in, making it easy to clean up.

Porcelain floor tile mimics stone so successfully that it's often difficult to tell the difference without looking at the label. Here, porcelain stone sets a natural tone for a four-season porch.

Quarry Tile

The name "quarry tile" is somewhat misleading because modern quarry tile isn't produced in a quarry. Instead, these tiles are made from red clay extruded through a die that makes them resemble cut stone. The die also creates a ribbed back on the tile to improve mortar adhesion.

The rough-hewn aspect of quarry tile makes it appealing and extremely slip resistant, but the open texture increases maintenance requirements. Quarry tile is often much more absorbent than glazed or porcelain tile, making it more prone to stains and mildew. Sealants must be added to increase this tile's durability and serviceability.

Quarry tile provides a rustic background for this unusual utility room. The color and tone complement the room's brickwork and stand in contrast to the elegant chandelier.

Photo courtesy of 18 Montana Tile & Stone Co./C. Price Wills

Natural Stone Tile

Natural stone tile has been a flooring material as long as there have been finished floors. Marble, granite, slate, and other more exotic stones are cut very precisely into tiles of various sizes that can be installed just like manufactured tile.

Because stone is a natural material, variations in color, texture, and markings are to be expected and are part of the charm of the material. Manufacturers do offer stone tiles with some added finish, though. In addition to polished, suppliers offer a variety of distressed and textured finishes that can be very attractive as well as slip resistant.

With the exception of granite, natural stone tends to be quite porous and requires periodic sealing to prevent staining. Also, not all types of stone are uniformly abrasion resistant, so check before making a purchase. Some stone is so soft that it can be very easily scratched by normal foot traffic.

Natural stone tile floors range from extremely formal and elegant to casual. Set in combination with decorative tile, this natural stone tile floor presents a rustic atmosphere in a western-style home.

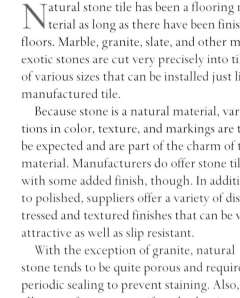

Terra-cotta Tile

Terra-cotta evokes images of rustic patios in Mexico or perhaps sunny piazzas on the Mediterranean. These images are quite appropriate because terra-cotta tile is very much a product of these regions. The tile is traditionally made by pressing unrefined clay into molds of various shapes and baking it (terra-cotta literally means "baked earth"). The color of the tile, from brown to red to yellow, is largely a result of the minerals unique to the local soil.

Machine-made terra-cotta tile is regular in shape and can be laid like standard tile, but traditional terra-cotta, especially handmade Mexican *saltillo* tile, has irregularities and uneven shapes and thus requires more care during installation. The variability and rustic character of the tile make up much of its appeal—and they make terra-cotta quite slip resistant.

Unglazed terra-cotta, which is porous and absorbent, should be treated with sealant before being used in wet locations.

Photo courtesy of Ceramic Tiles of Italy

Informal and earthy, terra-cotta can be recognized by its characteristic color and texture. Machine-made tile is consistent in size and shape, but handmade tile includes a wide range of shapes and textures.

Cement Body Tile

Photo courtesy of Buddy Rhodes Studio

Cement body tile differs from most other tile in that it is not made from kiln-fired clay. Cement tiles are merely little squares of concrete. That may sound simple, but the finished product can be made in nearly endless colors and textures because cement can be dyed, coated, and molded quite easily. It can even be finished to take on the appearance of marble or other stone. Cement tile can also be pressed with pronounced raised or relief designs.

Cement tile is an economical choice both for its low cost and great durability, but there are several caveats to keep in mind. Unfinished cement tile is highly porous and stains very easily. This also means that some cement tile is unsuitable for outdoor installations, as it may crack if it freezes. Cement tile should be treated periodically with a sealant to preserve its appearance and prevent mildew.

Durable and practical, cement body tile is also economical and attractive. It should be periodically sealed to maintain its appearance.

Mosaic Tile

Mosaics are an ancient and intricate art form. Using tiny colored clay tiles, artists have created incredible images and patterns on the floors, walls, and ceilings of buildings from Greek temples to Byzantine cathedrals. Today, the individual tiles are ceramic, porcelain, terracotta, stone, or other tile cut into small pieces. They are often mounted on a mesh backing so that large squares of many tiles can be installed at once. These squares may be a solid color or contain a pattern or image. Individual mosaic tiles are also available for making custom accents and mosaics.

The variety of patterns and designs available in prefabricated mosaic tile squares is extensive, and adding just a few squares to a floor or a wall has a striking effect.

Mosaic tile can be very low maintenance or it can require periodic application of sealant, depending on what the individual tiles are made of. All mosaic tile is generally quite slip resistant, no matter what material, because of the large number of grout lines.

Combining mosaic tile in a variety of colors and sizes produces elegant designs. Elaborate patterns can be deceptively easy to create with tile mounted to mesh backings. Even pre-arranged borders are widely available.

Decorative Tile

Individual porcelain and ceramic tiles painted with decorative patterns and images are available for use as borders or as accents in large designs.

A few decorative tiles can add a splash of color to an otherwise simple design. Large or repeating designs continued over a series of tiles can add interest to a field of plain tiles.

Photo courtesy of Ceramic Tiles of Italy

Small decorative tiles set at the corners of larger plain tiles creates a lively floor with a minimum of effort and expense.

Baseboards & Thresholds

Tile baseboards can be used in place of the original wooden ones. Baseboard tiles are larger tiles with a rounded top edge—called a bullnose—and a slightly wider base. Matching or complementary baseboard tiles connect a tile floor to a tiled wall.

A variety of wood, metal, and tile thresholds are available to smooth the transition from one flooring material to another. Metal thresholds rest on top of the two flooring materials and are easy to install but tend to collect dust. Wood and marble, the most common transitions between tile and other materials, are better choices.

Photo courtesy of Walker Zanger, Inc.

Baseboard tile smoothly connects tile walls to tile floors. With the addition of a border or liners, a baseboard can become a decorative element.

Wall Tile

Wall tile, unlike floor tile, is free from the burden of bearing weight or withstanding heavy traffic, and so can be thinner, have finer finishes, and, in some cases, be less expensive.

Wall tile layouts tend to have more exposed edges, so manufacturers often offer matching trim and border pieces with finished edges. Wall tile is generally self spacing—individual tiles have small flanges on each edge to help keep the spacing even.

You can use floor tile on walls, but since it is heavier, it tends to slide down during installation. Using battens while installing can help solve this problem. Fewer styles of matching trim tile are available for floor tile, which may make it difficult to conceal unfinished edges.

Wall tile should not be used on floors or countertops, however, because it will not stand up to much weight or sharp impacts. If you have concerns about a tile's suitability, ask your retailer or look for ratings by the American National Standards Institute or the Porcelain Enamel Institute (see page 25).

Wall tile can be a fairly inconspicuous wall covering or, if used in an elaborate design, it can become the focal point of a room. As with floor tiles, there are styles for every effect from subtle to bold, so envision the effect you want before you head to the tile store or home improvement center. This section provides information to help you select wall tile.

Photo courtesy of Crossville Porcelain Stone

Photo courtesy of Oceanside Glasstile™

Borders liven up walls and break up otherwise boring expanses of solid color (above).

Even plain wall tile in solid colors makes a bold statement when combined with accessories in similar or complementary colors (left).

A Word on Ratings

Most tile intended for walls comes labeled with a water absorption rating. As with floor tile, absorbent wall tile will be susceptible to mildew and mold and be difficult to clean. Tiles are rated non-vitreous, semi-vitreous, vitreous, and impervious, in increasing order of water resistance. Practically speaking, these ratings tell you whether your tile may require sealant or if it can be left as is. Non-vitreous and semi-vitreous do absorb noticeable amounts of water and may need to be sealed in damp rooms like bathrooms. Sealant can alter a tile's appearance, so test before you buy.

There are a few other ratings to consider when purchasing wall tile. Depending on where you buy tile, it may be graded from 1 to 3 for the quality of manufacturing. Grade 1 indicates standard grade, suitable for all installations. Second grade indicates minor glaze and size flaws, but the tile is structurally standard. Grade 3 tiles may be slightly irregular in shape and are decorative, suitable only for walls. Tiles with manufacturing irregularities may be more difficult to lay out and install precisely. If you live in a freeze zone and are looking for outdoor tile, you'll also want tile rated resistant to frost. If the frost-resistant rating is not on the package, the retailer should be able to tell you. Some colored tile may come with a graphic to indicate the degree of color variation from tile to tile—and in most cases it does vary somewhat.

Glazed Ceramic Tile

Glazed ceramic tiles intended for walls are thinner, softer versions of ceramic floor tiles. Because walls see less wear and tear than floors, wall tile often has thinner, less abrasion-resistant glaze. As a result, glazed wall tile is lighter, easier to cut, and generally cheaper than floor tile.

As with glazed ceramic floor tiles, wall tiles are available in dozens of shapes and sizes and in almost any color imaginable, as well as an impressive variety of textures and molded designs. Matching border and trim pieces are generally available for glazed ceramic wall tile designs.

Liners, listellos, and trim are widely available in glazed ceramic tile (above).

Metallic glazes create slightly reflective surfaces that are particularly suited to contemporary rooms.

26

Porcelain Tile

Porcelain wall tile is thinner and lighter than porcelain floor tile, but is otherwise identical. It is made of pressed fine white clay fired at a very high temperture, which gives it the hardness and imperviousness to moisture characteristic of porcelain.

As with ceramic wall tile, porcelain comes in a large assortment of shapes, sizes, colors, and patterns, including accompanying trim and border pieces. Like porcelain floor tile but unlike ceramic, the colors in porcelain wall tile are tinted rather than glazed, so colors generally run the full thickness of the tile, making scratches on the surface less noticeable.

Porcelain tile is impervious to moisture, which makes it perfect for bathrooms and other wet areas.

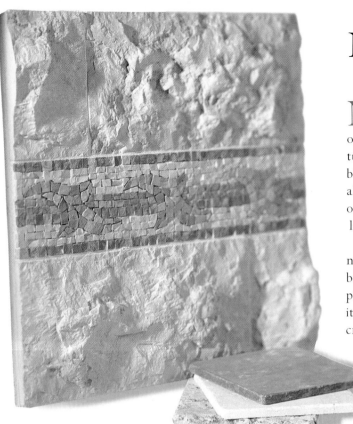

Natural Stone Tile

Natural stone tile—cut from marble, granite, slate, and other types of stone—has long been thought of as flooring material, but its natural patterns and textures are also suitable for walls in some situations. Tumbled stone tile has become extremely popular for walls all over the house. Polished and rough-cut stone tile are often used on fireplace surrounds and in other dry locations.

Stone tile is available in a variety of shapes and thicknesses. The thinner tiles are most appropriate for walls because they're easy to install. Some natural stone trim pieces are available, but the selection is somewhat limited. You may have to polish the edges of regular tile to create finished edges.

Unfinished rough stone is striking, but, with the exception of granite, absorbs water and stains easily if left unsealed. Light colored stone tends to stain and show dirt, so ask the retailer for guidance on sealing the stone you're considering.

Striking color combinations are made possible by the natural variations in stone.

Mosaic Tile

Colorful mosaics are as beautiful on walls as they are on floors. Small colorful tiles made of ceramic, porcelain, terra-cotta, or cement can be installed on walls to form patterns and pictures—or just to add a splash of color. The small size of mosaic tiles makes them particularly suited for neatly covering curved walls.

Mosaic tile can be expensive, but a few square feet of mosaic among a whole wall of simple ceramic or porcelain tiles creates an exciting decoration at little expense. You can also use shards of broken tile or even of china and porcelain dishes to create small mosaic accents on walls.

The maintenance requirements of mosaic tile depend on the materials used to make the tile, but, in general, mosaic tile walls are durable and resistant to moisture.

Mosaic tile can be used to create elaborate designs (above) or simple combinations (right) that allow the beauty of the materials to take center stage.

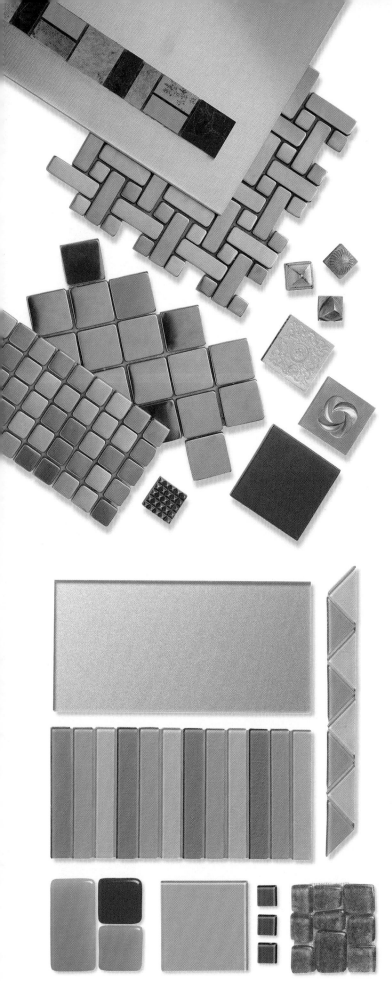

Metal & Glass Tile

Tiles made of stainless steel, brass, iron, and copper are an exciting alternative to clay-based tiles. They are quite expensive per square foot, but adding just a few metal tiles to a wall of glazed or porcelain tiles can have a big effect.

You install metal tiles just like standard tiles, and they are available in shapes and thicknesses to work in most layouts. They are available with smooth finishes, polished or unpolished, and with embossed designs. Some metals may weather and discolor with time and exposure to moisture.

Glass tile is another interesting option for walls (and, in some applications, floors). Glass tile is available in a variety of colors and degrees of translucency, as well as shapes and sizes.

Because most glass tile is translucent to some degree, it's important to use a white tile adhesive that won't affect the appearance of the tiles once they are installed. Glass is impervious to moisture, but it can be scratched and cracked, so it shouldn't be installed where it will get hit by swinging doors or scratched by general traffic.

Photo courtesy of Euro-Tile featuring Villi®Glas
opposite photo courtesy of Ceramic Tiles of Italy

Translucence and variations in color give glass tile character and appeal.

Art Tile

Tile making is an ancient art, and modern artisans continue the tradition with beautiful painted and embossed tiles.

Art tiles are available in as many designs, shapes, sizes, and colors as you can imagine. They make wonderful accents and borders for walls, and just a few eye-catching tiles will give a wall a distinctive appearance.

You can also create your own art tiles. Ceramic craft stores around the country offer facilities for painting and glazing your designs on blank tiles.

Because of their handcrafted finishes, art tiles can be less durable and resistant to scratches and moisture than most tile. They should be used only in areas where they will not be subject to excessive wear and tear or to moisture.

Handmade art tile ranges from original, hand-painted mosaics to tiles that are individually shaped and formed by hand. Some art tile is available through specialty tile shops, but many artisans offer their wares directly through the Internet. A simple search yields hundreds of alternatives.

Liners & Listellos

Borders and outlines are simple and effective ways to cap off tile designs, and there are several kinds of tile suited to the job. Liner tiles are very narrow tiles used to make lines and borders in tile designs. Solid-color liner tiles can be used to add a stripe of contrasting color to a tile layout, or they can outline a few art tiles, making the art tiles stand out against the field tiles. Liners are also available with printed or molded patterns.

Listellos are a similar kind of accessory tile. They have painted or molded patterns and often are slightly thicker than normal wall tile so as to stand out beyond the field tiles. Listellos can be used to finish a field of tile or to create a transition between one pattern or color and another. Listellos are particularly good for making chair rails.

Liners and listellos can be used to create interesting borders or to complete the edges of partial walls.

Trim tile provides easy, elegant ways to finish the edges and corners of walls and countertop projects.

Trim Tile

Many tiles designed for walls have matching trim pieces that conceal the exposed edges of field tile.

Tile with one edge that curves into the wall—called "bullnose" tile—is the most common type of trim tile and is used to finish the edges of partial walls. Trim tile is also available for tiling corners and making curves, especially on countertops and backsplashes.

Trim tile can do more than just hide rough edges, though. The right contrasting trim finishes a design elegantly.

Trim tile for borders is available in a variety of widths and styles. When planning a project, investigate available trim as part of the planning process.

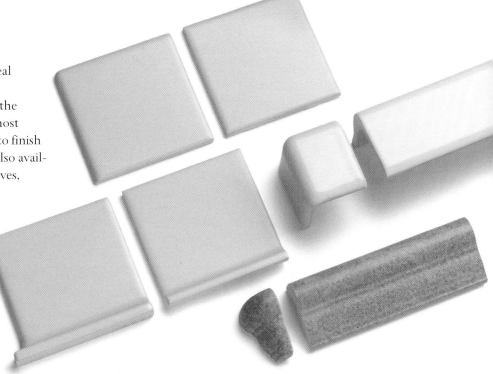

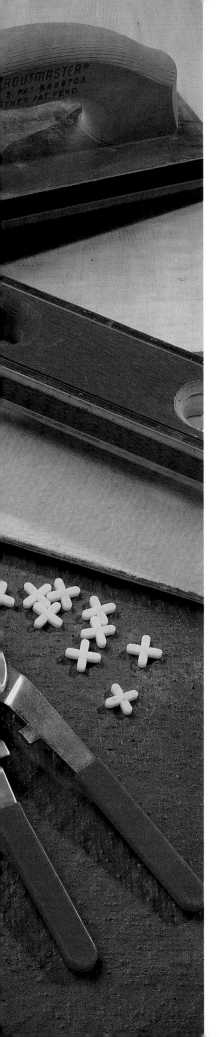

Tools &
Materials

End-cutting nippers

Heat gun

Hand maul

Flat pry bar

Chisel

Floor scraper

Tools for Removing Old Surfaces

Quality tools remove old surfaces faster and leave surfaces ready to accept new tile. Home centers and hardware stores carry a variety of products for surface removal. Look for tools with smooth, secure handles and correctly weighted heads for safety and comfort.

End-cutting nippers allow you to pull out staples remaining in the floor after carpeting is removed. This plier-like tool can also be used to break an edge on old tile so a chisel or pry bar can be inserted.

Heat guns are used to soften adhesives so vinyl base cove moldings and stubborn tiles can be pryed away from the wall. They are also used to remove old paint, especially when it is heavily layered or badly chipped.

Hand mauls are often used in combination with pry bars and chisels to remove old flooring and prepare surfaces for tile. They are helpful for leveling high spots on concrete floors and separating underlayments and subfloors.

Flat pry bars are used to remove wood base moldings from walls and to separate underlayments and floor coverings from subfloors. This tool is also effective for removing tiles set in mortar.

Chisels come in a variety of sizes for specific jobs. Masonry chisels are used with hand mauls to remove high spots in concrete. Cold chisels are used with hand mauls or hammers to pry tiles from mortar.

Floor scrapers are used to scrape and smooth patched areas on concrete floors and to pry up flooring, and scrape adhesives and backings from underlayments.

Tools for Repairing & Installing Substrates

Surfaces and substrates must be in good condition before new tile can be installed. Use the tools below to create stiff, flat surfaces that help prevent tiles from cracking and enhance the overall appearance of your finished project.

Straightedges are used to mark damaged areas of substrate for removal. They are also used to measure and mark replacement pieces for cutting.

Jig saws are handy when cutting notches, holes, and irregular shapes in new or existing substrates. They are also used to fit new substrate pieces to existing doorways.

Portable drills secure substrates to subfloors, with screws selected for the thickness and type of substrate used.

Circular saws are used to remove damaged sections of subfloor and cut replacement pieces to fit.

Straightedge

Jig saw

Circular saw

Portable drill

Tools for Installing Substrates

Depending upon your application, you may have to cut and install a substrate of cementboard, plywood, cork, backerboard, greenboard, or moisture membrane. Whichever your tiling project demands, the tools shown here will help you measure, score, cut, and install substrate material with precision.

Drywall square

Drywall squares are used to measure and mark substrates, such as cementboard, fiber/cementboard, and solation membrane. They can also be used as straightedge guides for scoring and cutting substrates with a utility knife.

Utility knives are usually adequate for scoring straight lines in wallboard, cementboard, fiber/cementboard, and for cutting isolation membrane substrates. However, because cementboard and fiber/cementboard are thick, hard substrates, utility knife blades must be replaced often for best performance.

Utility knife

Cementboard knives are the best choice for scoring cementboard and fiber/cementboard. The blades on these knives are stronger and wear better than utility knife blades when cutting rough surfaces.

Trowels are useful for applying leveler on existing floors and for applying thin-set mortar to substrates. Trowels can also be used to scrape away ridges and high spots after levelers or mortars dry.

Cementboard knife

Notched trowel

Straightedge

Level

Carpenter's square

Tools for Layout

Laying tile requires careful planning. Since tile is installed following a grid-pattern layout, marking perpendicular reference lines is essential to proper placement. Use the tools shown here to measure and mark reference lines for any type of tiling project.

Straightedges are handy for marking reference lines on small areas. They can also be used to mark cutting lines for partial tiles.

Levels are used to check walls for plumb and horizontal surfaces for level before tile is laid. Levels are also used to mark layouts for wall tile installations.

Carpenter's squares are used to establish perpendicular lines for floor tile installations.

Chalk lines are snapped to mark the reference lines for layouts.

Tape measures are essential for measuring rooms and creating layouts. They're also used to make sure that reference lines are perpendicular by using the 3-4-5 triangle method. (See page 83.)

Chalk line

Tape measure

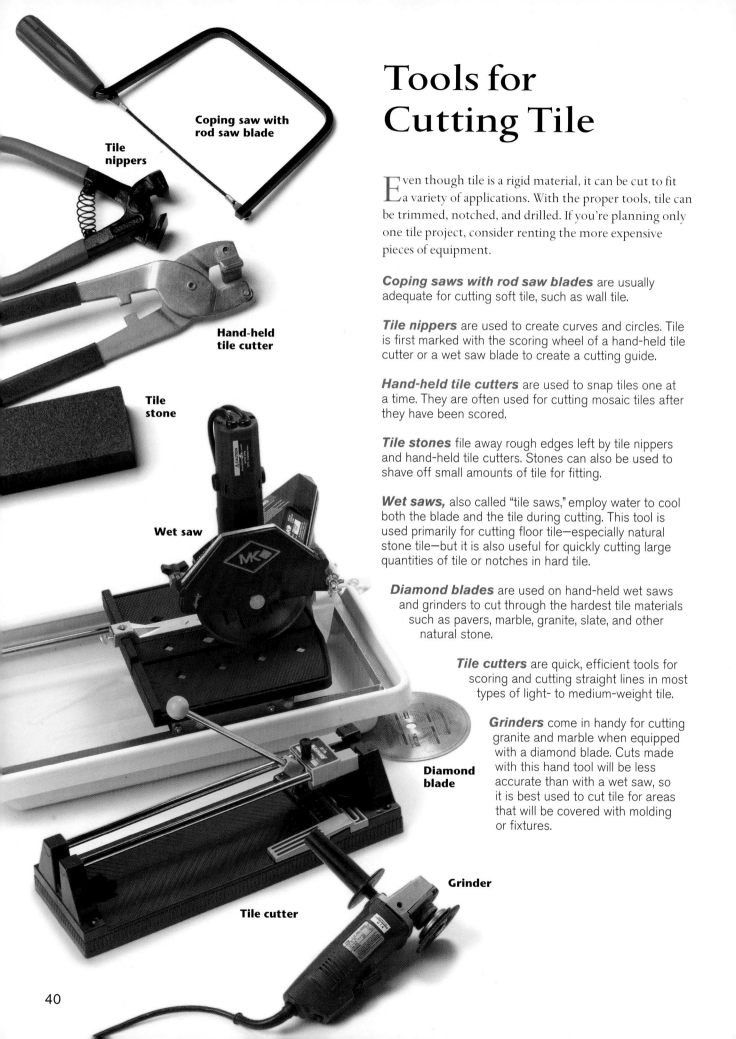

Tools for Cutting Tile

Even though tile is a rigid material, it can be cut to fit a variety of applications. With the proper tools, tile can be trimmed, notched, and drilled. If you're planning only one tile project, consider renting the more expensive pieces of equipment.

Coping saws with rod saw blades are usually adequate for cutting soft tile, such as wall tile.

Tile nippers are used to create curves and circles. Tile is first marked with the scoring wheel of a hand-held tile cutter or a wet saw blade to create a cutting guide.

Hand-held tile cutters are used to snap tiles one at a time. They are often used for cutting mosaic tiles after they have been scored.

Tile stones file away rough edges left by tile nippers and hand-held tile cutters. Stones can also be used to shave off small amounts of tile for fitting.

Wet saws, also called "tile saws," employ water to cool both the blade and the tile during cutting. This tool is used primarily for cutting floor tile—especially natural stone tile—but it is also useful for quickly cutting large quantities of tile or notches in hard tile.

Diamond blades are used on hand-held wet saws and grinders to cut through the hardest tile materials such as pavers, marble, granite, slate, and other natural stone.

Tile cutters are quick, efficient tools for scoring and cutting straight lines in most types of light- to medium-weight tile.

Grinders come in handy for cutting granite and marble when equipped with a diamond blade. Cuts made with this hand tool will be less accurate than with a wet saw, so it is best used to cut tile for areas that will be covered with molding or fixtures.

Coping saw with rod saw blade

Tile nippers

Hand-held tile cutter

Tile stone

Wet saw

Diamond blade

Tile cutter

Grinder

Tools for Setting & Grouting Tile

Tile spacers

Buff rag

Grout sponge

Grout sealer applicator

Foam brush

Rubber mallet

Needlenose pliers

Caulk gun

Grout float

Trowel

Notched trowel

Laying tile requires quick, precise work, so it's wise to assemble the necessary supplies before you begin. You don't want to search for a tool with wet mortar already in place. Most of the tools required for setting and grouting tile are probably already in your tool box, so take an inventory before you head to the home center or hardware store.

Tile spacers are essential for achieving consistent spacing between tiles. They are set at corners of laid tile and are later removed so grout can be applied.

Grout sponges, buff rags, foam brushes and grout sealer applicators are used after grout is applied. Grout sponges are used to wipe away grout residue, buff rags remove grout haze, and foam brushes and grout sealer applicators are for applying grout sealer.

Rubber mallets are used to gently tap tiles and set them evenly into mortar.

Needlenose pliers come in handy for removing spacers placed between tiles.

Caulk guns are used to fill expansion joints at the floor and base trim, at inside corners, and where tile meets surfaces made of other materials.

Grout floats are used to apply grout over tile and into joints. They are also used to remove excess grout from the surface of tiles after grout has been applied. For mosaic sheets, grout floats are handy for gently pressing tile into mortar.

Trowels are used to apply mortar to surfaces where tile will be laid and to apply mortar directly to the backs of cut tiles.

41

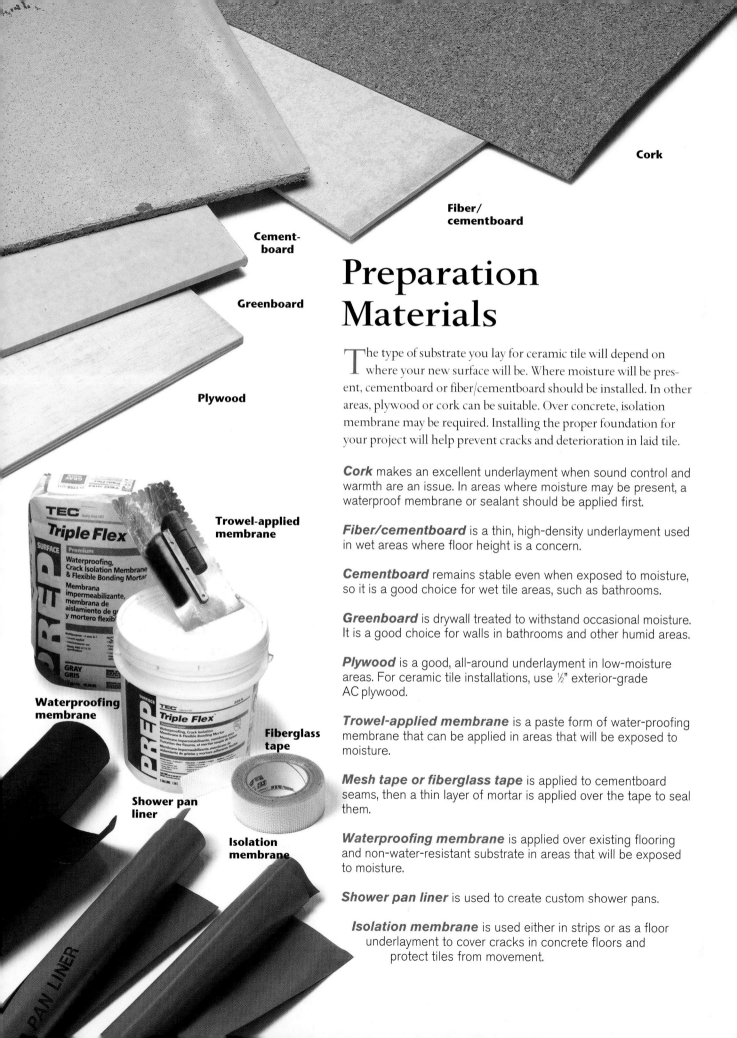

Cork

**Fiber/
cementboard**

**Cement-
board**

Greenboard

Plywood

**Trowel-applied
membrane**

**Waterproofing
membrane**

**Fiberglass
tape**

**Shower pan
liner**

**Isolation
membrane**

Preparation Materials

The type of substrate you lay for ceramic tile will depend on where your new surface will be. Where moisture will be present, cementboard or fiber/cementboard should be installed. In other areas, plywood or cork can be suitable. Over concrete, isolation membrane may be required. Installing the proper foundation for your project will help prevent cracks and deterioration in laid tile.

Cork makes an excellent underlayment when sound control and warmth are an issue. In areas where moisture may be present, a waterproof membrane or sealant should be applied first.

Fiber/cementboard is a thin, high-density underlayment used in wet areas where floor height is a concern.

Cementboard remains stable even when exposed to moisture, so it is a good choice for wet tile areas, such as bathrooms.

Greenboard is drywall treated to withstand occasional moisture. It is a good choice for walls in bathrooms and other humid areas.

Plywood is a good, all-around underlayment in low-moisture areas. For ceramic tile installations, use ½" exterior-grade AC plywood.

Trowel-applied membrane is a paste form of water-proofing membrane that can be applied in areas that will be exposed to moisture.

Mesh tape or fiberglass tape is applied to cementboard seams, then a thin layer of mortar is applied over the tape to seal them.

Waterproofing membrane is applied over existing flooring and non-water-resistant substrate in areas that will be exposed to moisture.

Shower pan liner is used to create custom shower pans.

Isolation membrane is used either in strips or as a floor underlayment to cover cracks in concrete floors and protect tiles from movement.

Materials for Setting & Grouting Tile

To ensure your tiling project lasts, it's important to set and grout the tile properly. Follow directions for mixing and applying mortars, fortifiers, and adhesives. Then seal grout to keep your tile beautiful and long-lasting.

Thin-set mortar is a cement-based adhesive that is purchased in dry form and prepared by adding liquid until a creamy consistency is achieved. Some mortars include a latex additive in the dry mix. Other mortars require a liquid latex additive.

Grout fills the spaces between tiles and is available in pre-tinted colors to match your tile. Grout width should be considered a decorative element of your tile project.

Latex fortifier is a liquid added to mortar to strengthen its bonding power. Some mortar powders include fortifier in the dry mix.

Grout sealer is applied with a sponge brush to ward off stains and make tile maintenance easier.

Wall tile mastic is used to install base-trim tile.

Wall and floor tile adhesive is available in pre-mixed formulas. Thin-set mortar is, however, recommended for most flooring installations.

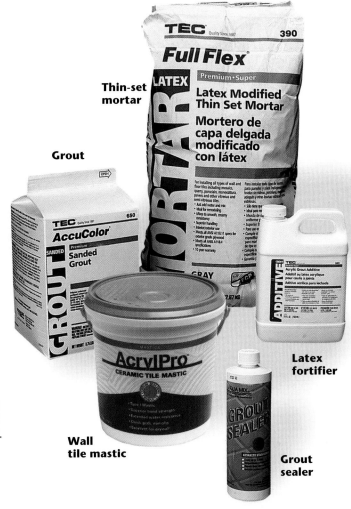

Thin-set mortar

Grout

Latex fortifier

Wall tile mastic

Grout sealer

Floor tile adhesive

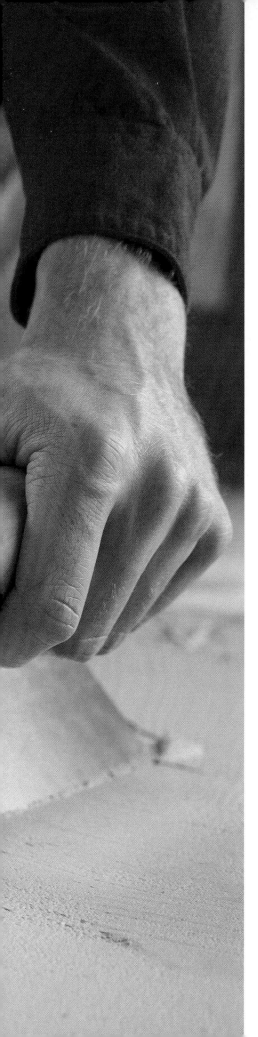

Preparation

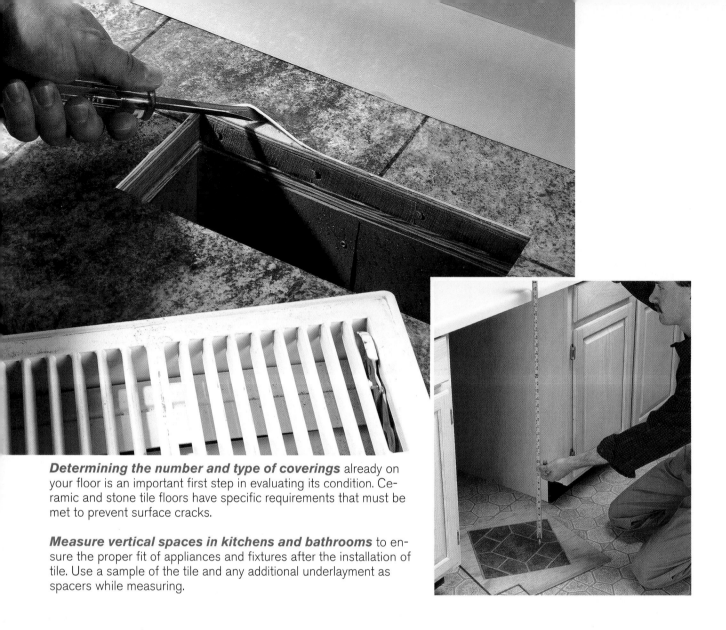

Determining the number and type of coverings already on your floor is an important first step in evaluating its condition. Ceramic and stone tile floors have specific requirements that must be met to prevent surface cracks.

Measure vertical spaces in kitchens and bathrooms to ensure the proper fit of appliances and fixtures after the installation of tile. Use a sample of the tile and any additional underlayment as spacers while measuring.

Evaluating & Preparing Floors

The most important step in the success of your tile flooring project is evaluating and preparing the area. A well-done tile installation can last a lifetime—poor preparation can lead to a lifetime of cracked grout and broken tile headaches.

Because of the weight of ceramic and stone tile, it is important to assess the condition and placement of the joists, subfloor, and underlayment. Most tile installation cannot be done over existing flooring without the addition of underlayment. Check with your tile dealer for the specific requirements of the tile or stone you have chosen.

Though it may initially seem like more work, it is important to remove bathroom fixtures and vanities and non-plumbed kitchen islands for your floor tile project. Not only will this eliminate a great deal of cutting and fitting, it will allow you more flexibility in future remodeling choices.

Start by removing any fixtures or appliances in the work area, then baseboards, then the old flooring. Shovel old flooring debris through a window and into a wheelbarrow to speed up removal work. Cover doorways with sheet plastic to contain debris and dust during the removal process. Keep the dust and dirt from blowing throughout your house by covering air and heat vents with sheet plastic and masking tape.

Tips for Preparing Trim for Tile Installation

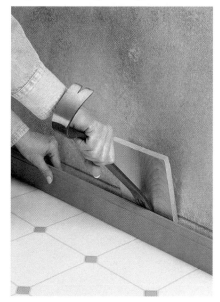

To remove baseboards, place a scrap board against the wall to avoid damaging the drywall. Remove the baseboard using a pry bar placed against the scrap board. Pry the baseboard at all nail locations. Number the baseboards as they are removed.

To prepare door jambs, measure the height of your underlayment and tile and mark the casing. Using a jamb saw, cut the casing at the mark.

To test the height of the door jamb, slide a piece of flooring under the door jamb to make sure it fits easily.

Anatomy of Your Floor

A typical wood-frame floor consists of several layers that work together to provide the required structural support and desired appearance. At the bottom of the floor are the joists, the 2 × 10 or larger framing members that support the weight of the floor. Joists are typically spaced 16" apart on-center. The subfloor is nailed to the joists. Most subfloors installed in the 1970s or later are made of ¾" tongue-and-groove plywood, but in older homes, the subfloor often consists of 1"-thick wood planks nailed diagonally across the floor joists. On top of the subfloor, most builders place a ½" plywood underlayment. For many types of floor coverings, adhesive or mortar is spread on the underlayment prior to installing the floor covering.

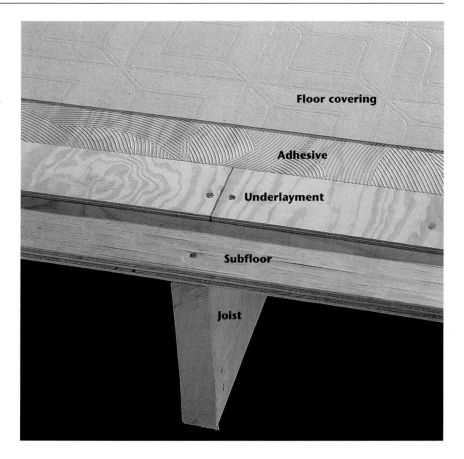

Floor covering

Adhesive

Underlayment

Subfloor

Joist

Removing a Toilet

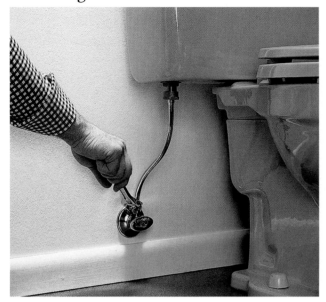

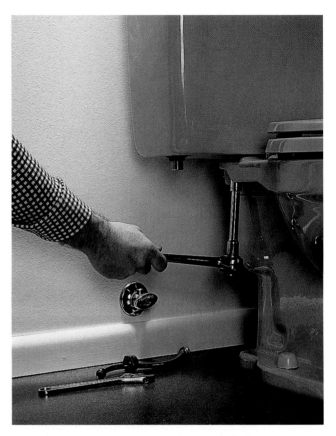

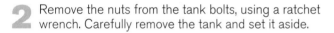

1 Turn off the water at the shutoff valve and flush the toilet to empty the tank. Use a sponge to soak up remaining water in the tank and bowl. Disconnect the supply tube, using an adjustable wrench.

2 Remove the nuts from the tank bolts, using a ratchet wrench. Carefully remove the tank and set it aside.

3 Pry off the floor bolt trim caps, then remove the nuts from the floor bolts. Rock the bowl from side to side to break the seal, then lift the toilet from the bolts and set it aside. Wear rubber gloves while cleaning up any water that spills from the toilet trap.

4 Scrape the old wax from the toilet flange, and plug the drain opening with a damp rag so sewer gas doesn't escape into the house. If you're going to reinstall the old toilet, clean the old wax and plumber's putty from around the horn and base of the toilet.

Removing Sinks

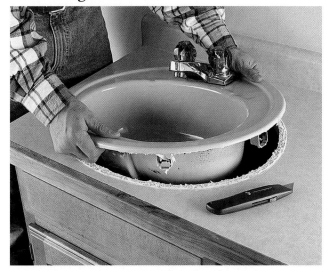

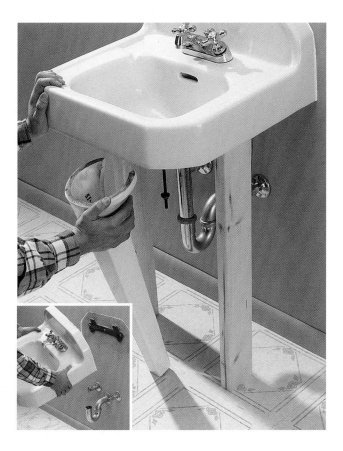

Self-rimming sink: Disconnect the plumbing, then slice through any caulk or sealant between the sink rim and the countertop, using a utility knife. Lift the sink off the countertop.

Pedestal sink: Disconnect the plumbing. If the sink and pedestal are bolted together, disconnect them. Remove the pedestal first, supporting the sink from below with 2 × 4s. Slice through any caulk or sealant. Lift the sink off the wall brackets.

Removing Vanities

1 Detach any mounting hardware, located underneath the countertop inside the vanity.

2 Slice through any caulk or sealant between the wall and the countertop. Remove the countertop from the vanity, using a pry bar if necessary.

3 Remove the screws or nails (usually driven through the back rail of the cabinet) that anchor the vanity to the wall.

Use a floor scraper to remove resilient flooring products and to scrape off leftover adhesives or backings. The long handle provides leverage and force, and it allows you to work in a comfortable standing position. A scraper will remove most flooring, but you may need to use other tools to finish the job.

Removing Floor Coverings

When removing old floor coverings, thorough and careful removal work is essential to the quality of a new floor tile or stone installation.

The difficulty of flooring removal depends on the type of floor covering and the method that was used to install it. Carpet and perimeter-bond vinyl are generally quite easy to remove, and vinyl tiles are relatively simple. Full-spread sheet vinyl can be difficult to remove, however, and removing ceramic tile is a lot of work.

With any removal project, be sure to keep your tool blades sharp and avoid damaging the underlayment if you plan to reuse it. If you'll be replacing the underlayment, it may be easier to remove the old underlayment along with the floor covering (see pages 54 through 55).

Resilient flooring from before 1986 might contain asbestos, so consult an asbestos containment expert or have a sample tested before beginning removal. Even if no asbestos is present, wear a good quality dust mask.

EVERYTHING YOU NEED

Tools: floor scraper, utility knife, spray bottle, wallboard knife, wet/dry vacuum, heat gun, hand maul, masonry chisel, flat pry bar, end-cutting nippers.

Materials: liquid dishwashing detergent.

Removing Sheet Vinyl

1 Remove base moldings, if necessary. Use a utility knife to cut old flooring into strips about a foot wide.

2 Pull up as much flooring as possible by hand, gripping the strips close to the floor to minimize tearing.

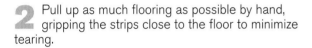

3 Cut stubborn sheet vinyl into strips about 5" wide. Starting at a wall, peel up as much of the floor covering as possible. If the felt backing remains, spray a solution of water and liquid dishwashing detergent under the surface layer to help separate the backing. Use a wallboard knife to scrape up particularly stubborn patches.

4 Scrape up the remaining sheet vinyl and backing, using a floor scraper. If necessary, spray the backing again with the soap solution to loosen it. Sweep up the debris, then finish the cleanup with a wet/dry vacuum. *Tip:* Fill the vacuum with about an inch of water to help contain dust.

Removing Vinyl Tiles

1 Remove base moldings, if necessary. Starting at a loose seam, use a long-handled floor scraper to remove tiles. To remove stubborn tiles, soften the adhesive with a heat gun, then use a wallboard knife to pry up the tile and scrape off the underlying adhesive.

2 Remove stubborn adhesive or backing by wetting the floor with a water/detergent mixture, then scraping with a floor scraper.

Removing Ceramic Tile

1 Remove base moldings, if necessary. Knock out tile using a hand maul and masonry chisel. If possible, start in a space between tiles where the grout has loosened. Be careful when working around fragile fixtures, such as drain flanges.

2 If you plan to reuse the underlayment, use a floor scraper to remove any remaining adhesive. You may have to use a belt sander with a coarse sanding belt to grind off stubborn adhesive.

Removing Carpet

1 Using a utility knife, cut around metal threshold strips to free the carpet. Remove the threshold strips with a flat pry bar.

2 Cut the carpet into pieces small enough to be easily removed. Roll up the carpet and remove it from the room, then remove the padding. *Note:* Padding often is stapled to the floor, and usually will come up in pieces as you roll it up.

3 Using end-cutting nippers or pliers, remove all staples from the floor. *Tip:* If you plan to lay new carpet, do not remove the tackless strips unless they are damaged.

Variation: To remove glued-down carpet, first cut it into strips with a utility knife, then pull up as much material as you can. Scrape up the remaining cushion material and adhesive with a floor scraper.

Remove underlayment and floor covering as though they were a single layer. This is an effective removal strategy with any floor covering that is bonded to the underlayment.

Removing Underlayment

Flooring contractors routinely remove the underlayment along with the floor covering before installing new flooring. This saves time and makes it possible to install new underlayment that is ideally suited to ceramic and stone tile. Do-it-yourselfers using this technique should make sure they cut flooring into pieces that can be easily handled.

Warning: This floor removal method releases flooring particles into the air. Be sure the flooring you are removing does not contain asbestos.

EVERYTHING YOU NEED

Tools: goggles, gloves, circular saw with carbide-tipped blade, flat pry bar, reciprocating saw, wood chisel.

Tip: Examine fasteners to see how the underlayment is attached. Use a screwdriver to expose the heads of the fasteners. If the underlayment has been screwed down, you will need to remove the floor covering and then unscrew the underlayment.

1 Remove base moldings, if necessary. Adjust the cutting depth of a circular saw to equal the combined thickness of your floor covering and underlayment. Using a carbide-tipped blade, cut the floor covering and underlayment into squares measuring about 3 ft. square. Be sure to wear safety goggles and gloves.

2 Use a reciprocating saw to extend cuts close to the edges of walls. Hold the blade at a slight angle to the floor, and try not to damage walls or cabinets. Do not cut deeper than the underlayment. Use a wood chisel to complete cuts near cabinets.

3 Separate the underlayment from the subfloor, using a flat pry bar and hammer. Remove and discard the sections of underlayment and floor covering immediately, watching for exposed nails.

Variation: If your existing floor is ceramic tile over plywood underlayment, use a hand maul and masonry chisel to chip away the tile along the cutting lines before making the cuts.

Before installing new underlayment and floor covering, refasten any sections of loose subfloor to floor joists, using deck screws.

Repairing Subfloors

A solid, securely fastened subfloor minimizes floor movement and prevents grout and tile cracking. After removing the old underlayment, inspect the subfloor for loose seams, moisture damage, cracks, and other flaws. Bulges and dips may require repairs to the joists, or simply application of a leveler.

Concrete floors also need to be evaluated for cracks and holes, which can be repaired, and dips and bulges, which can be filled with concrete leveler. Concrete floors may also require an isolation membrane (see page 63) to further protect tiles from cracking.

EVERYTHING YOU NEED

Tools: trowel, straightedge, framing square, drill, circular saw, cat's paw, wood chisel, ratchet wrench, vacuum, gage rake, hammer, tape measure.

Materials: 2" deck screws, floor leveler, plywood, 2 × 4 lumber, 10d common nails, lag screws, paint roller.

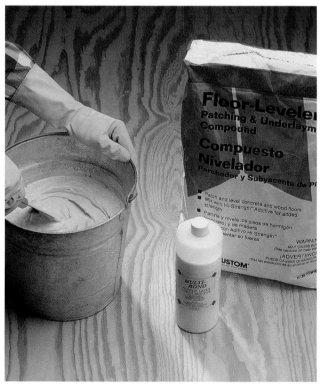

Floor leveler is used to fill in dips and low spots in plywood subfloors. Mix the leveler according to the manufacturer's directions, adding a latex or acrylic additive.

Applying Floor Leveler

1 Mix the leveler according to the manufacturer's directions, then spread it onto the subfloor with a trowel. Build up the leveler in thin layers to avoid overfilling the area.

2 Check with a straightedge to make sure the filled area is even with the surrounding area; if necessary, apply more leveler. Allow the leveler to dry, then shave off any ridges with the edge of a trowel, or sand it smooth, if necessary.

Replacing a Section of Subfloor

1 Cut out damaged areas of the subfloor. Use a framing square to mark a rectangle around the damage—make sure two sides of the rectangle are centered over floor joists. Remove nails along the lines, using a cat's paw. Make the cut using a circular saw adjusted so the blade cuts through only the subfloor. Use a chisel to complete the cuts near walls.

2 Remove the damaged section, then nail two 2 × 4 blocks between the joists, centered under the cut edges for added support. If possible, endnail the blocks from below; otherwise toenail them from above, using 10d nails.

3 Measure the cutout section, then cut a patch to fit, using material of the same thickness as the original subfloor. Fasten the patch to the joists and blocks, using 2" deck screws spaced about 5" apart.

Reinforcing Floor Joists

Sister joist

3" lag screw

Cross beam

Temporary post

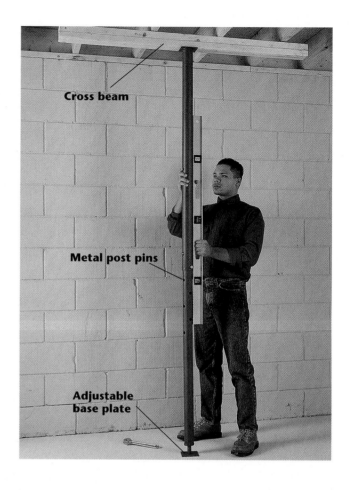

Cross beam

Metal post pins

Adjustable base plate

To reinforce floor joists, attach a sister joist alongside the existing joist, using 3" lag screws. The sister joist should run the full length of the original floor joist. Sister joists should be installed wherever existing joists are damaged, and may be required under floor areas that will support the additional weight of bathtubs or whirlpools.

Install a support post and cross beam below a sagging floor. Adjust the post to rough height, then position the post so it is plumb. Raise the post by turning the threaded base plate; pressure will hold the post and beam in place. Raise no more than ¼" per week, until floor above is level. Building codes may restrict the use of adjustable posts, so consult an inspector.

Reducing a Bulging Joist

1 Check the area with a level to find the highest point. Move the level to different points, noting the gap between the floor and the ends of the level. Mark the highest point of the bulge, and measure from an element that extends below the floor, such as an exterior wall or a heating duct. Use this measurement to mark the high point on the bulging joist from below the floor.

2 From the bottom edge, make a straight cut into the problem joist below the high point mark, using a reciprocating saw. Make the cut ¾ the depth of the joist. Allow several weeks for the joist to relax and straighten, checking the floor periodically with a level. Don't load the floor above the joist with excessive weight.

3 When the joist has settled, reinforce it by nailing a board of the same size to the joist. Make the reinforcement piece at least 6 ft. long, and drive 16d common nails in staggered pairs, 12" apart. Drive a row of three nails on either side of the cut in the joist.

Patching Concrete Floors

1 Clean the floor with a vacuum, and remove any loose or flaking concrete with a masonry chisel and hammer. Mix a batch of vinyl floor patching compound, following manufacturer's directions. Apply the compound using a smooth trowel, slightly overfilling the cavity. Smooth the patch flush with the surface.

2 After the compound has cured fully, use a floor scraper to scrape the patched areas smooth.

Applying Floor Leveler

1 Remove any loose material and clean the concrete thoroughly; the surface must be free of dust, dirt, oils, and paint. Apply an even layer of concrete primer to the entire surface, using a long-nap paint roller. Let the primer dry completely.

2 Following the manufacturer's instructions, mix the floor leveler with water. The batch should be large enough to cover the entire floor area to the desired thickness (up to 1"). Pour the leveler over the floor.

3 Distribute the leveler evenly, using a gage rake or spreader. Work quickly: The leveler begins to harden in 15 minutes. Use a trowel to feather the edges and create a smooth transition with an uncovered area. Let the leveler dry for 24 hours.

Installing Underlayment

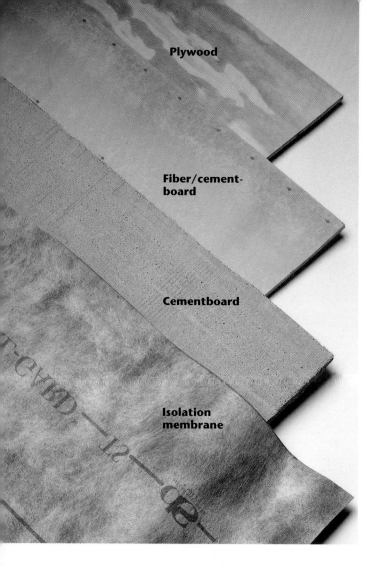

Plywood

Fiber/cementboard

Cementboard

Isolation membrane

Embossing leveler is a mortar-like substance used for preparing well-adhered resilient flooring or ceramic tile for use as an underlayment. Mix the leveler according to the manufacturer's directions, and spread it thinly over the floor with a flat-edged trowel. Wipe away any excess, making sure all dips and indentations are filled. Work quickly—embossing leveler begins to set in 10 minutes. After the leveler dries, scrape away ridges and high spots with the trowel.

Ceramic and natural stone tile floors often require an underlayment that stands up to moisture, such as cementboard. If you will use your old flooring as underlayment, apply an embossing leveler to prepare it for the new installation (see below, left).

When installing new underlayment, make sure it is securely attached to the subfloor in all areas, including below all movable appliances. Notch the underlayment to fit room contours. Around door casings and other moldings, undercut the moldings and insert the underlayment beneath them.

Plywood is typically used as an underlayment for vinyl flooring and for ceramic tile installations in dry areas. For ceramic tile, use ½" exterior-grade AC plywood. Do not use particleboard, oriented-strand board, or treated lumber as underlayment for tile.

Fiber/cementboard is a thin, high-density underlayment used under ceramic tile in situations where floor height is a concern. (For installation, follow the steps for cementboard, on page 62.)

Cementboard is used exclusively for ceramic or stone tile installations. It remains stable even when exposed to moisture and is therefore the best underlayment to use in areas likely to get wet, such as bathrooms.

Isolation membrane is used to protect ceramic tile installations from movement that may occur on cracked concrete floors. It is often used to cover individual cracks, but it can also be used over an entire floor. Isolation membrane also is available in a liquid form that can be poured over the project area.

EVERYTHING YOU NEED

Tools: drill, circular saw, wallboard knife, power sander, ¼" notched trowel, straightedge, utility knife, jig saw with carbide blade, ⅛" notched trowel, flooring roller.

Materials: plywood underlayment, 1" deck screws, floor-patching compound, latex additive, thin-set mortar, 1½" galvanized deck screws, cementboard, fiberglass-mesh wallboard tape.

Installing Plywood Underlayment

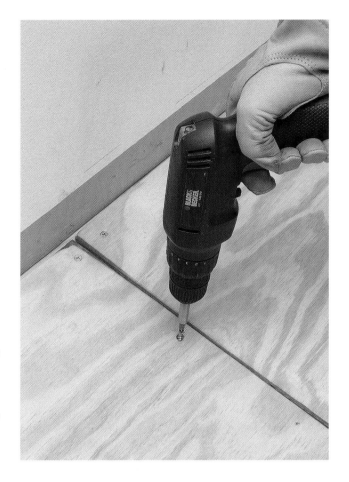

1 Begin by installing a full sheet of plywood along the longest wall, making sure the underlayment seams will not be aligned with the subfloor seams. Fasten the plywood to the subfloor, using 1" deck screws driven every 6" along the edges and at 8" intervals in the field of the sheet.

2 Continue fastening sheets of plywood to the subfloor, driving the screw heads slightly below the underlayment surface. Leave ¼" expansion gaps at the walls and between sheets. Offset seams in subsequent rows.

3 Using a circular saw or jig saw, notch plywood to meet existing flooring in doorways, then fasten the notched sheets to the subfloor.

4 Mix floor-patching compound and latex or acrylic additive, according to the manufacturer's directions. Spread it over seams and screw heads with a wallboard knife.

5 Let the patching compound dry, then sand the patched areas, using a power sander.

Installing Cementboard

1 Mix thin-set mortar (see page 43) according to the manufacturer's directions. Starting at the longest wall, spread the mortar on the subfloor in a figure-eight pattern, using a ¼" notched trowel. Spread only enough mortar for one sheet at a time. Set the cementboard on the mortar with the rough side up, making sure the edges are offset from the subfloor seams.

2 Fasten the cementboard to the subfloor, using 1½" galvanized deck screws driven every 6" along edges and 8" throughout the sheet. Drive the screw heads flush with the surface. Continue spreading mortar and installing sheets along the wall.

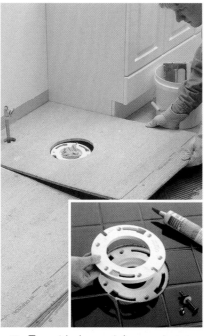

3 Cut cementboard pieces as necessary, leaving a ⅛" gap at all joints and a ¼" gap along the room perimeter. For straight cuts, use a utility knife to score a line through the fiber-mesh layer just beneath the surface, then snap the board along the scored line.

4 To cut holes, notches, or irregular shapes, use a jig saw with a carbide blade. Continue installing cementboard sheets to cover the entire floor. *Inset:* A flange extender or additional wax ring may be needed to ensure a proper toilet installation after additional layers of underlayment have been installed in a bathroom.

5 Place fiberglass-mesh wallboard tape over the seams. Use a wallboard knife to apply thin-set mortar to the seams, filling the gaps between sheets and spreading a thin layer of mortar over the tape. Allow the mortar to cure for two days before starting the tile installation.

Installing Isolation Membrane

1 Thoroughly clean the subfloor, then apply thin-set mortar (see page 43) with a ⅛" notched trowel. Start spreading the mortar along a wall in a section as wide as the membrane and 8 to 10 ft. long. *Note:* For some membranes, you must use a bonding material other than mortar. Read and follow label directions.

2 Roll out the membrane over the mortar. Cut the membrane to fit tightly against the walls, using a straightedge and utility knife.

3 Starting in the center of the membrane, use a heavy flooring roller (available at rental centers) to smooth out the surface toward the edges. This frees trapped air and presses out excess bonding material.

4 Repeat steps 1 through 3, cutting the membrane as necessary at the walls and obstacles, until the floor is completely covered with membrane. Do not overlap the seams, but make sure they are tight. Allow the mortar to cure for two days before installing the tile.

Installing a Floor-warming System

Floor-warming systems require very little energy to run and are designed to heat ceramic tile floors only; they generally are not used as sole heat sources for rooms.

A typical floor-warming system consists of one or more thin mats containing electric resistance wires that heat up when energized, like an electric blanket. The mats are installed beneath the tile and are hardwired to a 120-volt GFCI circuit. A thermostat controls the temperature, and a timer turns the system on or off automatically.

The system shown in this project includes two plastic mesh mats, each with its own power lead that is wired directly to the thermostat. The mats are laid over a concrete floor and then covered with thin-set adhesive and ceramic tile. If you have a wood subfloor, install cementboard before laying the mats.

A crucial part of installing this system is to perform several resistance checks to make sure the heating wires have not been damaged during shipping or during the installation.

Electrical service required for a floor-warming system is based on size. A smaller system may connect to an existing GFCI circuit, but a larger one will need a dedicated circuit; follow the manufacturer's requirements.

To order a floor-warming system, contact the manufacturer or dealer. In most cases, you can send them plans and they'll custom-fit a system for your project area.

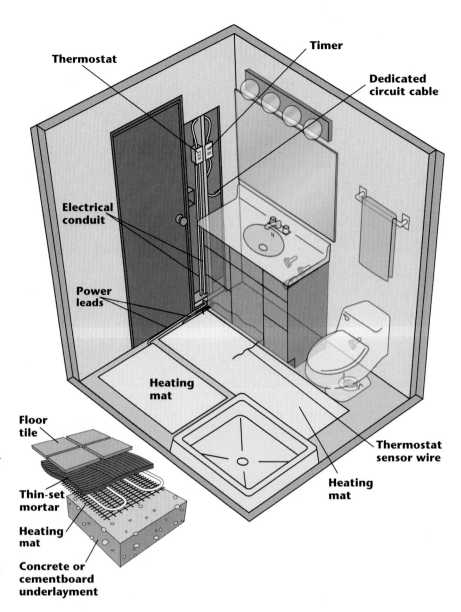

Labels: Thermostat, Timer, Dedicated circuit cable, Electrical conduit, Power leads, Heating mat, Floor tile, Thin-set mortar, Heating mat, Concrete or cementboard underlayment, Thermostat sensor wire, Heating mat

EVERYTHING YOU NEED

Tools: multi-tester, drill, plumb bob, chisel, tubing cutter, combination tool, vacuum, chalk line, grinder, hot-glue gun, fish tape, tile tools (page 41).

Materials: floor-warming system, 2½" × 4" double-gang electrical box, single-gang electrical box, ½"-dia. thin-wall conduit, setscrew fittings, 12-gauge NM cable, cable clamps, double-sided tape, electrical tape, insulated cable clamps, wire connectors, tile materials (page 43).

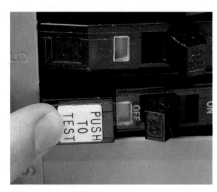

Floor-warming systems must be installed on a circuit with adequate amperage and a GFCI breaker (some systems have built-in GFCIs). Smaller systems may tie into an existing circuit, but larger ones need a dedicated circuit. Follow local building and electrical codes that apply to your project.

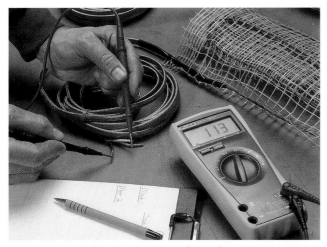

1 Check the resistance value (ohms) of each heating mat, using a digital multi-tester. Record the reading. Compare your reading to the factory-tested reading noted by the manufacturer—your reading must fall within the acceptable range determined by the manufacturer. If it does not, the mat has been damaged and should not be installed; contact the manufacturer for assistance.

2 Install electrical boxes for the thermostat and timer at an accessible location. Remove the wall surface to expose the framing, then locate the boxes approximately 60" from the floor, making sure the power leads of the heating mats will reach the double-gang electrical box. Mount a 2½"-deep × 4"-wide double-gang electrical box (for the thermostat) to the stud closest to the determined location, and a single-gang electrical box (for the timer) on the other side of the stud.

3 Use a plumb bob to mark points on the bottom plate directly below the two knockouts on the thermostat box. At each mark, drill a ½" hole through the top of the plate, then drill two more holes as close as possible to the floor through the side of the plate, intersecting the top holes. (The holes will be used to route the power leads and thermostat sensor wire.) Clean up the holes with a chisel to ensure smooth routing.

4 Cut two lengths of ½" thin-wall electrical conduit to fit between the thermostat box and the bottom plate, using a tubing cutter. Place the bottom end of each length of conduit about ¼" into the holes in the bottom plate, and fasten the top end to the thermostat box, using a setscrew fitting. *Note:* If you are installing three or more mats, use ¾" conduit instead of ½".

(continued next page)

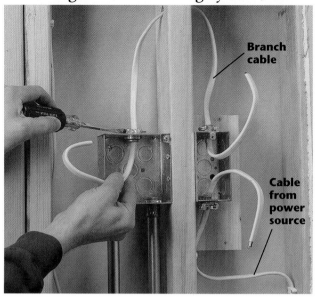

5 Run 12-gauge NM electrical cable from the service panel (power source) to the timer box. Attach the cable to the box with a cable clamp, leaving 8" of extra cable extending from the box. Drill a ⅝" hole through the center of the stud, about 12" above the boxes. Run a short branch cable from the timer box to the thermostat box, securing both ends with clamps. The branch cable should make a smooth curve where it passes through the stud.

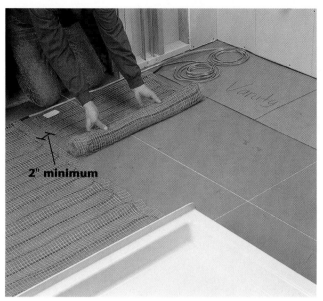

6 Vacuum the floor thoroughly. Plan the ceramic tile layout and snap reference lines for the tile installation (pages 83 to 84). Spread the heating mats onto the floor with the power leads closest to the electrical boxes. Position the mats 3" to 6" away from walls, showers, bathtubs, and toilet flanges. You can lay the mats into the kick space of a vanity, but not under the vanity cabinet or over expansion joints in a concrete slab. Set the edges of the mats close together, but do not overlap them: The heating wires in one mat must be at least 2" from the wires in the neighboring mat.

7 Confirm that the power leads still reach the thermostat box. Secure the mats to the floor, using strips of double-sided tape spaced every 24". Make sure the mats are lying flat with no wrinkles or ripples. Press down firmly to secure the mats to the tape.

8 Create recesses in the floor for the connections between the power leads and the heating-mat wires, using a grinder or a cold chisel and hammer. These insulated connections are too thick to lay under the tile and must be recessed to within ⅛" of the floor. Clean away any debris, and secure the connections in the recesses with a bead of hot glue.

9 Thread a steel fish tape down one of the conduits, and attach the ends of the power leads to the fish tape, using electrical tape. Pull the fish tape and leads up through the conduit. Disconnect the fish tape, and secure the leads to the box with insulated cable clamps. Cut off the excess from the leads, leaving 8" extending from the clamps.

10 Feed the heat sensor wire down through the remaining conduit and weave it into the mesh of the nearest mat. Use dabs of hot glue to secure the sensor wire directly between two blue resistance wires, extending it 6" to 12" into the mat. Test the resistance of the heating mats with a multi-tester (step 1, page 65) to make sure the resistance wires have not been damaged. Record the reading.

11 Install the ceramic floor tile (pages 116 to 120). Use thin-set mortar as an adhesive, and spread it carefully over the floor and mats with a ⅜" × ¼" square-notched trowel. Check the resistance of the mats periodically during the tile installation. If a mat becomes damaged, clean up any exposed mortar and contact the manufacturer. When the installation is complete, check the resistance of the mats once again and record the reading.

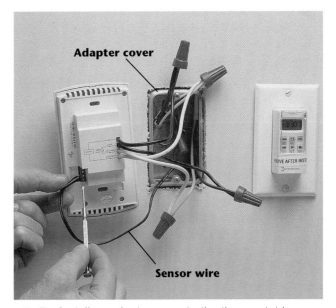

Adapter cover

Sensor wire

12 Install an adapter cover to the thermostat box, then patch the wall opening with drywall. Complete the wiring connections for the thermostat and timer, following the manufacturer's instructions. Attach the sensor wire to the thermostat setscrew connection. Apply the manufacturer's wiring labels to the thermostat box and service panel. Mount the thermostat and timer. Complete the circuit connection at the service panel or branch connection. After the flooring materials have fully cured, test the system.

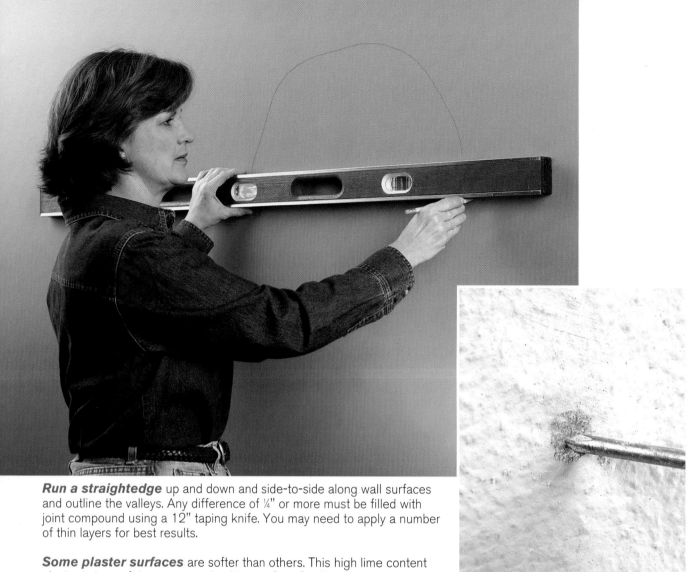

Run a straightedge up and down and side-to-side along wall surfaces and outline the valleys. Any difference of ¼" or more must be filled with joint compound using a 12" taping knife. You may need to apply a number of thin layers for best results.

Some plaster surfaces are softer than others. This high lime content plaster is too soft to serve as a backing surface for tile.

Evaluating & Preparing Walls

The substrate for wall tiles must be stable; that is, it must not expand and contract in response to changes in temperature or humidity. For this reason, you need to strip all wallpaper before tiling, even if the paper has been painted. Similarly, remove any type of wood paneling before tiling a wall. Even painted walls need some preparation. For example, paint that's likely to peel needs to be sanded thoroughly before the project starts.

Smooth, concrete walls can be tiled, but the concrete has to be prepared. Scrub it with a concrete cleaner, then apply a concrete bonding agent. Use a grinder to smooth any unevenness. Install an isolation membrane (see pages 76 to 77) to keep the tile from cracking if the walls crack, which is common.

Brick or block walls are a good substrate for tiling, but the surface is not smooth enough to be tiled without additional preparation. Mix extra portland cement into brick mortar and apply a smooth, even skim coat to the walls and let it dry thoroughly before beginning the tile project.

Existing tile can be tiled over as long as the glaze has been roughened enough for the adhesive to adhere properly. Remember, though, that the new tile will protrude quite a way from the wall. You'll need to accommodate for this on the edges and around receptacles, switches, windows or doors, and other obstacles.

In some cases, you'll find that it's easiest to remove the old substrate and install new (see pages 72 to 75). Even if you're working with an appropriate substrate in good condition, you will need to evaluate the wall to make sure it is plumb and flat, and fix surface flaws before you begin your wall tiling project.

Patching Holes

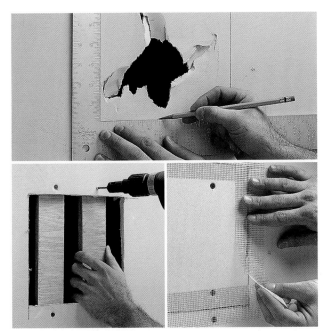

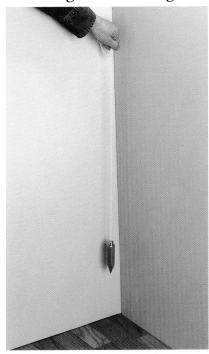

Patching small holes: Fill smooth holes with spackle, then sand, then smooth. Cover ragged holes with a repair patch, then apply two coats of spackle or wallboard compound. Use a damp sponge or wet sander to smooth the repair area, then sand when dry, if necessary.

Patching large holes: Draw cutting lines around the hole, then cut away the damaged area, using a wallboard saw. Place plywood strips behind the opening and drive wallboard screws to hold them in place. Drive screws through the patch and into the backers. Cover the joints with wallboard tape and finish with compound.

Checking & Correcting Out-of-plumb Walls

1 Use a plumb bob to determine if corners are plumb. A wall more than ½" out of plumb should be corrected before tiling.

2 If the wall is out of plumb, use a long level to mark a plumb line the entire height of the wall. Remove the wall covering from the out-of-plumb wall.

3 Cut and install shims on all the studs to create a new, plumb surface for attaching backing materials. Draw arrows at the shim high-points to mark for drywall screw placement.

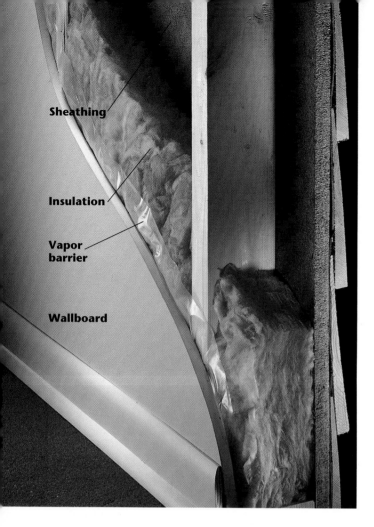

Sheathing

Insulation

Vapor barrier

Wallboard

Removing Wall Surfaces

You may have to remove and replace interior wall surfaces before starting your tiling project. Most often, the material you'll be removing is wallboard, but you may be removing plaster or ceramic tile. Removing wall surfaces is a messy job, but it is not difficult. Before you begin, shut off the power and inspect the wall for wiring and plumbing.

Make sure you wear appropriate safety gear—glasses and dust masks—since you will be generating dust and small pieces of debris. Use plastic sheeting to close off doorways and air vents to prevent dust from spreading throughout the house. Protect floor surfaces and the bathtub with rosin paper securely taped down. Dust and debris will find their way under drop cloths and will quickly scratch your floor or tub surfaces.

EVERYTHING YOU NEED

Tools: utility knife, pry bar, circular saw with demolition blade, straightedge, maul, masonry chisel, reciprocating saw with bimetal blade, heavy tarp, hammer, protective eyewear, dust mask.

Removing Wallboard

1 Remove baseboards and other trim, and prepare the work area. Make a ½"-deep cut from floor to ceiling, using a circular saw. Use a utility knife to finish the cuts at the top and bottom and to cut through the taped horizontal seam where the wall meets the ceiling surface.

2 Insert the end of a pry bar into the cut near one corner of the opening. Pull the pry bar until the wallboard breaks, then tear away the broken pieces. Take care to avoid damaging the wallboard outside the project area.

Removing Plaster

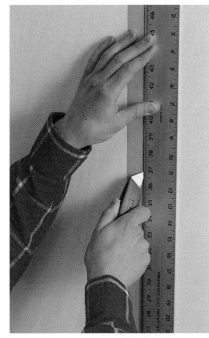

1 Remove baseboards and other trim and prepare the work area. Score the cutting line several times with a utility knife, using a straightedge as a guide. The line should be at least ⅛" deep.

2 Break the plaster along the edge by holding a scrap piece of 2 × 4 on edge just inside the scored line, and rapping it with a hammer. Use a pry bar to remove the remaining plaster.

3 Cut through the lath along the edges of the plaster, using a reciprocating saw or jig saw. Remove the lath from the studs, using a pry bar.

Removing Ceramic Wall Tile

1 Be sure the floor is covered with a heavy tarp, and the electricity and water are shut off. Knock a small starter hole into the bottom of the wall, using a maul and masonry chisel.

2 Begin cutting out small sections of the wall by inserting a reciprocating saw with a bimetal blade into the hole, and cutting along grout lines. Be careful when sawing near pipes and wiring.

3 Cut the entire wall surface into small sections, removing each section as it is cut. Be careful not to cut through studs.

Installing & Finishing Wallboard

Regular wallboard is an appropriate backer for ceramic tile in dry locations. Greenboard, a moisture resistent form of wallboard, is good for kitchens and the dry areas of bathrooms. Tub and shower surrounds and kitchen backsplashes should have a cementboard backer.

Wallboard panels are available in 4 × 8-ft. or 4 × 10-ft. sheets, and in ⅜", ½", and ⅝" thicknesses. For new walls, ½" thick is standard.

Install wallboard panels so that seams fall over the center of framing members, not at sides. Use all-purpose wallboard compound and paper joint tape to finish seams.

EVERYTHING YOU NEED

Tools: tape measure, utility knife, wallboard T-square, 6" and 12" wallboard knives, 150-grit sanding sponge, screw gun.

Materials: wallboard, wallboard tape, 1¼" coarse-thread wallboard screws, wallboard compound, metal inside corner bead.

Score wallboard face paper with a utility knife, using a drywall T-square as a guide. Bend the panel away from the scored line until the core breaks, then cut through the back paper (inset) with a utility knife, and separate the pieces.

1 Install panels with their tapered edges butted together. Fasten with 1¼" wallboard screws, driven every 8" along the edges, and every 12" in the field. Drive screws deep enough to dimple surface without ripping face paper (inset).

2 Finish the seams by applying an even bed layer of wallboard compound over the seam, about ⅛" thick, using a 6" taping knife.

3 Center the wallboard tape over the seam and lightly embed it into the compound, making sure it's smooth and straight.

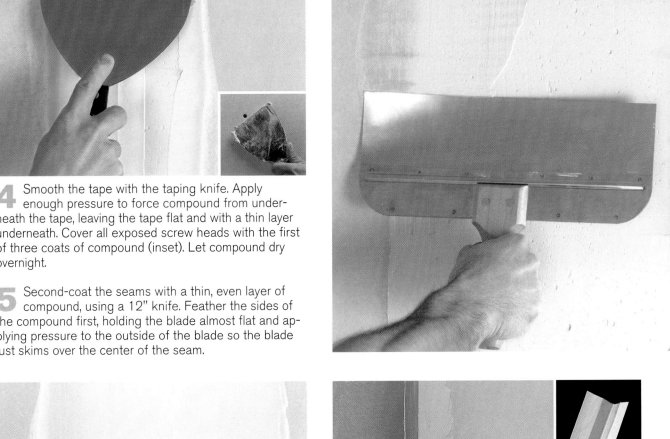

4 Smooth the tape with the taping knife. Apply enough pressure to force compound from underneath the tape, leaving the tape flat and with a thin layer underneath. Cover all exposed screw heads with the first of three coats of compound (inset). Let compound dry overnight.

5 Second-coat the seams with a thin, even layer of compound, using a 12" knife. Feather the sides of the compound first, holding the blade almost flat and applying pressure to the outside of the blade so the blade just skims over the center of the seam.

6 After feathering both sides, make a pass down the center of the seam, leaving the seam smooth and even, the edges feathered out even with the wallboard surface. Completely cover the joint tape. Let the second coat dry, then apply a third coat, using the 12" knife. After the third coat dries completely, sand the compound lightly with a wallboard sander or a 150-grit sanding sponge.

Tip: Finish any inside corners, using paper-faced metal inside corner bead to produce straight, durable corners with little fuss. Embed the bead into a thin layer of compound, then smooth the paper with a taping knife. Apply two finish coats to the corner, then sand the compound smooth.

Installing Cementboard

Use tile backer board as the substrate for tile walls in wet areas. Unlike wallboard, tile backer won't break down and cause damage if water gets behind the tile. The three basic types of tile backer are cementboard, fiber-cement board, and Dens-Shield.

Though water cannot damage either cementboard or fiber-cement board, it can pass through them. To protect the framing members, install a water barrier of 4-mil plastic or 15# building paper behind the backer.

Dens-Shield has a waterproof acrylic facing that provides the water barrier. It cuts and installs much like wallboard, but it requires galvanized screws to prevent corrosion and must be sealed with caulk at all untaped joints and penetrations.

EVERYTHING YOU NEED

Tools: utility knife, T-square, drill with a small masonry bit, hammer, jig saw with a bimetal blade, wallboard knife, stapler, drill.

Materials: 4-mil plastic sheeting, cementboard, 1¼" cementboard screws, cementboard joint tape, latex-portland cement mortar.

Common tile backers are cementboard, fiber-cement board, and Dens-Shield. Cementboard is made from portland cement and sand reinforced by an outer layer of fiberglass mesh. Fiber-cement board is made similarly, but with a fiber reinforcement integrated throughout the panel. Dens-Shield is a water-resistant gypsum board with a waterproof acrylic facing.

Cementboard

Fiber-cement board

Dens-Shield

1 Staple a water barrier of 4-mil plastic sheeting or 15# building paper over the framing. Overlap seams by several inches, and leave the sheets long at the perimeter. *Note:* Framing for cementboard must be 16" on-center; steel studs must be 20-gauge.

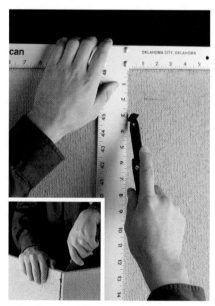

2 Cut cementboard by scoring through the mesh just below the surface, using a utility knife or carbide-tipped cutter. Snap the panel back, then cut through the back-side mesh (inset). *Note:* For tile applications, the rough face of the board is the front.

3 Make cutouts for pipes and other penetrations by drilling a series of holes through the board, using a small masonry bit. Tap the hole out with a hammer or a scrap of pipe. Cut holes along edges with a jig saw and bimetal blade.

4 Install the sheets horizontally. Where possible, use full pieces to avoid cut-and-butted seams, which are difficult to fasten. If there are vertical seams, stagger them between rows. Leave a ⅛" gap between sheets at vertical seams and corners. Use spacers to set the bottom row of panels ¼" above the tub or shower base. Fasten the sheets with 1¼" cementboard screws, driven every 8" for walls and every 6" for ceilings. Drive the screws ½" from the edges to prevent crumbling. If the studs are steel, don't fasten within 1" of the top track.

5 Cover the joints and corners with cementboard joint tape (alkali-resistant fiberglass mesh) and latex-portland cement mortar (thin-set). Apply a layer of mortar with a wallboard knife, embed the tape into the mortar, then smooth and level the mortar.

Variation: Finishing Cementboard

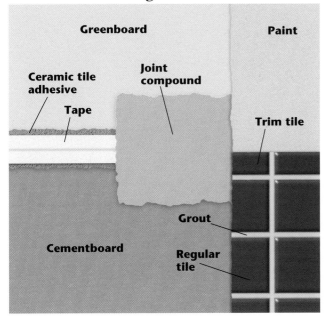

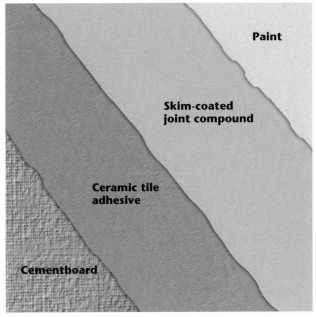

To finish a joint between cementboard and greenboard, seal the joint and exposed cementboard with ceramic tile adhesive, a mixture of four parts adhesive to one part water. Embed paper joint tape into the adhesive, smoothing the tape with a tape knife. Allow the adhesive to dry, then finish the joint with at least two coats of all-purpose wallboard joint compound.

To finish small areas of cementboard that will not be tiled, seal the cementboard with ceramic tile adhesive, a mixture of four parts adhesive to one part water, then apply a skim-coat of all-purpose wallboard joint compound, using a 12" wallboard knife. Then paint the wall.

Plastic sheeting, sheet membrane, building paper, and trowel-applied membrane are all options for adding waterproofing to walls. Isolation membranes in strips or sheets also protect tile surfaces from cracking caused by small movements in the underlayment.

Installing Wall Membranes

Wall membranes may provide waterproofing or isolation from small underlayment movement, or both. Because water does not sit on wall surfaces as it does on floors, waterproofing of walls is not as critical. In most cases, plastic sheeting or building paper behind cement backer board is sufficient. Saunas and steam rooms may need additional waterproofing.

Isolation membrane comes in roll- or trowel-on forms as well as in sheet form. It can be applied to existing cracks or potential areas of movement. Check the product directions for the maximum width crack or expansion joint that can be spanned and the type of substrate on which

it can be used.

It is important to apply isolation membrane to concrete walls to prevent hairline cracks from being transferred outward to the tile or grout surface. Some products combine waterproofing and isolation properties. The tile adhesive is applied directly to the isolation membrane after it has cured.

Be sure to check for compatibility between the roll- or trowel-on membranes and your particular application needs. Fountains and pools have specific waterproofing needs—check with your tile dealer if you plan on using wall tile for a pool wall.

A water barrier of 4-mil plastic sheeting can be stapled to studs before installing cementboard or fiber-cement board.

Building paper (15#) can also be used as a water barrier behind cementboard and fiber-cement board. Start from the bottom and install horizontally so each layer overlaps the previous one by two inches.

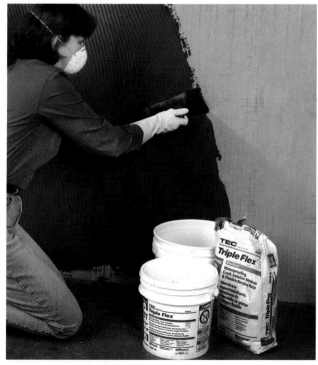

Waterproofing/isolation membranes are an easy way to add waterproofing and crack protection to existing walls. This application is especially suited to smooth, solid concrete surfaces. The tile adhesive is applied directly to the membrane after it dries.

Isolation membrane may be used on wall and ceiling surfaces in areas such as steam rooms and saunas that have extreme temperature fluctuation and high humidity. The membrane is typically installed with mortar, but some membranes must be used with a specific bonding agent.

Planning a Tile Project

79

Laying Out Floor Projects

Once you have a stable, firm, smooth substrate in place (see pages 52 to 63), the next step is laying out the project. While it might be tempting to go directly to laying the tile, resist the temptation. Planning is a very important step in the process and one that pays off in the long run. There are few things more frustrating than running into issues that could have been avoided through a little more attention to detail on the front end. A tile floor essentially is a giant grid, and imperfections can be quite obvious, especially if the grout contrasts sharply with the tile.

Good layouts start with accurate measurements and detailed scale drawings. Use these drawings to experiment with potential layouts until you're satisfied. Try to:
- Center the tile within the room and keep the final tiles at opposite sides equal in size.
- Minimize the number of cuts required.
- Disguise disparities in rooms that are not square.

Laying out borders, diagonal sets, or running bonds involves a few special considerations that are also discussed in the following pages.

Drawing Layouts

It's not necessary to draw layouts for projects in small, square rooms with no tricky issues. On the other hand, drawings are helpful for projects in rooms that have more than four corners or are more than an inch out of square, and for projects that involve several adjacent rooms.

To start, measure the room. Figure out a scale that's easy to use—one square per tile for larger-scale graph paper or four squares per tile on smaller-scale graph paper—and draw the room. Make several copies of the drawing so you can experiment with layouts without redoing it.

Next, lay out at least 10 tiles with spacers and measure them. Add the thickness of one grout line and divide the total by 10 to calculate the exact size of one tile with grout. Using this calculation and the same scale as you used for the room diagram, draw layouts until you find one that works. Sometimes there's no way to avoid narrow tiles at the edges. In that case, plan to put them along the least visible wall in the room or in areas that will be covered with furniture or fixtures.

Confirm your calculations by testing the layout. No matter how careful you are, it's possible to make mistakes when you're working with drawings and measurements. It's much better to discover any miscalculations before setting any tile or spreading any mortar. Lay out one complete row of full-sized tile in at least two directions. Adjust the layout as necessary.

If the layout is complicated or involves lots of cuts, it's worth the time to dry-fit the entire floor.

Measuring a Room

To get accurate room measurements, start in a corner of the room and measure along the wall to the opposite corner. Do this for each wall, writing down the measurements as you go. When measuring to locate permanent obstacles or fixtures, pick a point and take all measurements from it. That way you'll have a constant reference point when you diagram the room.

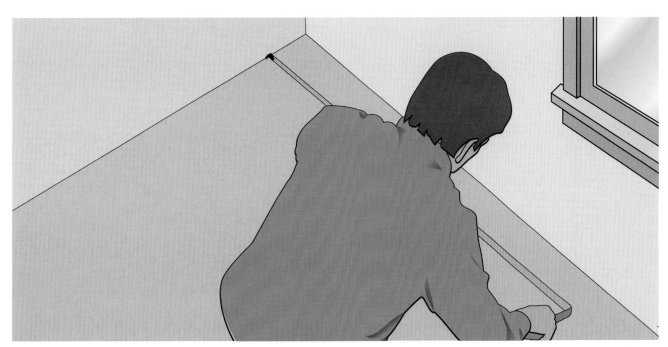

Check for square by measuring a corner. On one wall, mark a spot 3 feet from the corner; on the other wall, mark a spot 4 feet from the corner. Measure between the marks. If the distance between the marks is exactly 5 feet, the room is square. For greater accuracy in larger rooms, use multiples of 3, 4, and 5 such as 6, 8, and 10 or 9, 12, and 15.

Laying Out Your Project

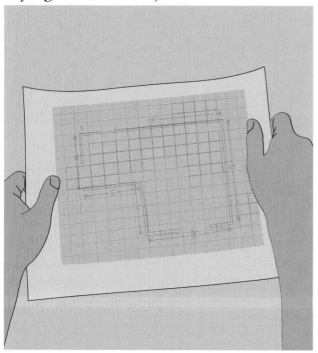

Diagram the entire room, drawing it to scale including any permanent fixtures such as cabinets and stairways. Draw possible tile layouts, at the same scale as your room drawing, on transparency paper and place them over the room diagram. Experiment with layouts until you find a successful arrangement.

Make a story stick to help you estimate how many tiles will fit in a given area. Lay out a row of tile, with spacers, and set an 8-ft.-long 1 × 2 next to it. (Position the end of the 1 × 2 in the center of a grout line.) Holding the board in place, mark the edges of each grout line.

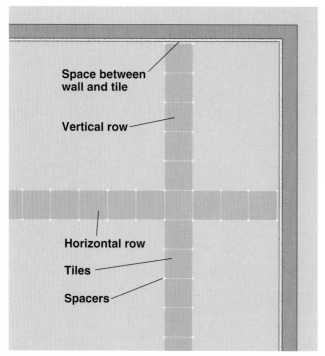

Space between wall and tile

Vertical row

Horizontal row

Tiles

Spacers

Test the layout by setting out one vertical and one horizontal row of tile, all the way to the walls in both directions.

Dry-lay the tile if you're working with a complex layout, tiling around a series of obstacles, or setting tiles on the diagonal. You may find that you need to shift the layout slightly to keep from cutting very small tile for edges or corners.

Planning Expansion Joints

What is an expansion joint and why might you need one? An expansion joint allows materials to move without cracking. This is important because building materials, including tile and stone, expand and contract with changes in temperature. In new construction, the house itself also settles over time. Plumbing pipes expand and contract quite a bit, and they sometimes move as water flows through them. Most of the time, these movements go unnoticed, but even small movements add up across large spaces. Plus, walls move at different rates than the floors below them. To avoid problems, create expansion joints in large tile floors, between walls and floors, and around all water pipes.

On very large floors, it's best to install contractor-style expansion joints, but for most do-it-yourself projects, a simple caulk joint works well. Just fill the joints with caulk and let it dry before you grout the surrounding tile. On a floor that extends more than 30 feet in any direction, fill a grout line with silicone caulk; between adjoining rooms, fill a grout line in the middle of the doorway with caulk. If you tile a wall and the adjoining floor, caulk the joint between them. Finally, always cut holes around plumbing pipes large enough to leave a gap at least ⅛" wide between the tile and the pipe. Fill the gap with silicone caulk.

Establishing Reference Lines for Floor Projects

Reference lines are used as guides for the first tiles laid. Before you snap these lines, think about where to start tiling. The goal is to work it out so that you don't need to step on recently laid tile in order to continue working. It often makes sense to start in the middle of a room, but not always—sometimes it's better to start a few feet from a wall and work your way across the room. If a room has only one door, start at the far end and move toward the door. Give some thought to the issue and make sure you don't tile yourself into a corner!

Another way to help keep the tile straight is by using a batten, which is nothing more than a long, straight board used as a guide. A piece of plywood works well if you maintain the factory edge. Just position the board and tack it in place, using several screws. Butt the first row of tile up to it and leave it in place until the mortar starts to dry. Remove the batten and continue setting tile. Maintaining even spacing will maintain the straight lines.

Marking Reference Lines for Straight Sets

1 Position a reference line (X) by measuring between opposite sides of the room and marking the center of each side. Snap a chalk line between these marks.

2 Measure and mark the centerpoint of the chalk line. From this point, use a framing square to establish a second line perpendicular to the first. Snap a second reference line (Y) across the room.

Marking Reference Lines for Diagonal Sets

1 Snap reference lines that meet in the exact center of the room. Make sure the lines are perpendicular, then mark a point on each line precisely the same distance from the center.

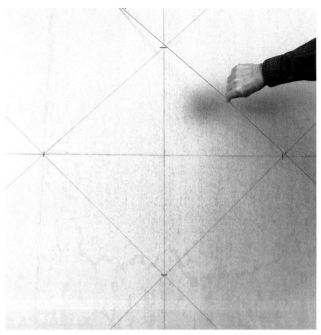

2 Snap lines to connect the marked points. The sides of the resulting square will be tilted at a 45° angle to the room. Use the square to create working lines for laying out the room.

Marking Reference Lines for Running Bond Sets

1 Snap perpendicular reference lines as described on page 83. Dry-fit a few tiles side by side, using spacers. Offset the rows by a measurement that's equal to one-half the length of the tile and one-half the width of the grout line. Measure the total width of the dry-fitted section.

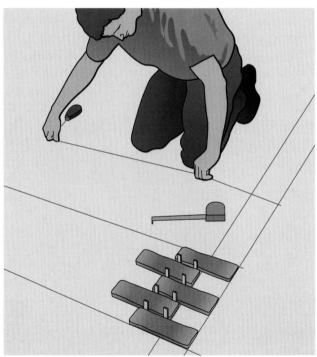

2 Use this measurement to snap a series of equally spaced parallel lines to help keep your tiles straight during installation. (Running-bond layouts are most effective with rectangular tiles.)

Planning Borders & Design Areas

A border can divide a floor into sections or it can define a design area such as the one shown at right. You can create a design inside the border by merely turning the tiles at a 45° angle, by installing decorative tiles, or by creating a mosaic such as the one shown on pages 130 to 135. Such designs should cover between 25 and 50 percent of the floor. If the design is too small, it'll get lost in the floor. If it's too big, it'll be distracting.

Determine the size and location of the border on graph paper, then transfer those measurements onto the floor. A dry run with the border and field tile is essential.

The tile is installed in three stages. The border is placed first, followed by outside field tile, then the tile within the border.

Photo courtesy of Crossville Porcelain Stone

1 Measure the length and width of the room in which you'll be installing the border.

2 Transfer the measurements onto paper by making a scale drawing of the room. Include the locations of cabinets, doors, permanent fixtures, and furniture.

(continued next page)

3 Determine the size of the border you want. Bordered designs should be between ¼ and ½ the area of the room. Draw the border on transparency paper, using the same scale as the room drawing.

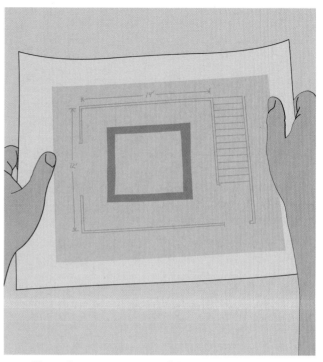

4 Place the transparency of the border over the room drawing. Move it around to find the best layout. Tape the border transparency in place over the room drawing. Draw perpendicular lines through the center of the border and calculate the distance from the center lines to the border.

5 Transfer the measurements from the border transparency onto your floor, starting with your center lines. Snap chalk lines to establish your layout for the border.

6 Lay out the border along the reference lines in a dry run. Do a dry run of the field tiles along the center lines inside and outside of the border. Make any adjustments, if necessary.

Laying Out Wall Projects

Wall projects can be challenging because walls are so rarely plumb and true. In some cases, that means the walls themselves need to be adjusted before the tile portion of the project begins. Most of the time, though, it simply means being aware of the issues and working around them as discussed in the following pages. (If your walls need work before you begin tiling them, consult pages 68 to 77 for ideas and information.)

Layout is critical to successful wall projects. Start with accurate measurements and draw the room to scale.

Use the drawing to experiment with potential arrangements. The goal is to arrive at a layout that gives the walls a balanced, symmetrical look.

- Center the tile within the room and keep the final tiles at opposite sides equal in size.
- Minimize the number of cuts required and avoid cutting very narrow pieces of tile.
- Disguise disparities on walls that are not square.
- Plan effective placement of borders, liners, and trim.

Drawing Layouts

Check the walls and corners to see if they're plumb. Make any adjustments necessary before beginning your tile project.

Measure the walls, paying particular attention to the placement of windows, doors, and permanent fixtures. Use these measurements to create a scale drawing of each wall to be tiled.

It may not be necessary to draw layouts for small, simple projects, but it's a good idea if you're tiling more than one wall, creating designs or borders, or working with walls that aren't plumb or a room that's out of square by more than an inch.

Start by checking to see whether the walls are plumb. Place a carpenter's level along the edge of a straight board, then place the board against the walls and on the floor at the bottom of the walls. If a wall is out of square by more than ¼" per 8 feet, you'll need to add moldings, build up the wall with joint compound, or trim the tiles in a way that makes the imperfection less obvious. (See pages 68 to 73 for details.) Check outside corners for plumb and make careful note of any problems.

Now, measure and draw the walls on graph paper, including windows, doors, and permanent fixtures such as bathtubs. (Figure out a scale that's easy to use—one square per tile for larger-scale graph paper or four squares per tile on smaller-scale graph paper.) Make several copies of the drawing so you can experiment with layouts without redrawing it.

Double check the size of your tile, including borders or accent tiles, and begin evaluating layouts. The goal is to make the room look balanced and to place cut tile in the least visible positions. For example, if the height of a wall above a sink or bathtub can't be covered in full tile, it's best to put cut tile on the bottom row so that the top row (which is more visible) is composed of full tile. If you're adding accents, position them so that the repeating pattern is even or at least balanced across the wall.

Lay out your tiles, accents, and trim. Take measurements of the tile layout.

Draw your tile layout to scale on the wall drawing to establish your reference lines.

Testing Layouts

Establishing perpendicular reference lines is a critical part of every tile project, including wall projects. To create these lines, measure and mark the midpoint at the top and bottom of the wall, and then again along each side. Snap chalk lines between opposite marks to create your vertical and horizontal centerlines. Use the 3-4-5 triangle method to make sure the lines are drawn correctly (see page 81). Adjust the lines until they are exactly perpendicular.

Next, do a dry run of your proposed layout, starting at the center of the wall and working toward an adjoining wall. If the gap between the last full tile and the wall is too narrow, adjust your starting point. Continue to dry-fit tile along the walls, paying special attention to any windows, doors, or permanent fixtures in the wall. If you end up with very narrow tiles anywhere, adjust the reference lines (and your layout) to avoid them. It's best not to cut tiles by more than half.

If your wall has an outside corner, start your dry run there. Place bullnose tiles over the edges of the adjoining field tiles. If this results in a narrow gap at the opposite wall, install trimmed tile next to the bullnose edge to even out or avoid the gap.

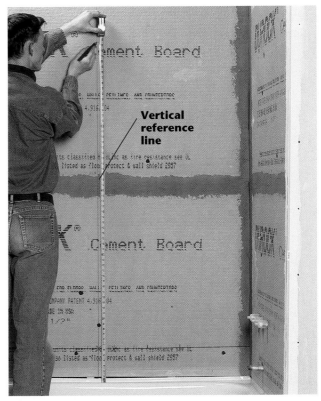

Measure and mark the horizontal and vertical midpoints of the wall, then snap chalk lines between sets of opposite marks. Use the 3-4-5 triangle method (see page 81) to make sure the lines are perpendicular to one another.

(continued next page)

1 Attach a batten to the wall along your horizontal reference line, using screws. Dry-fit tiles on the batten, aligning the middle tile with the vertical centerline.

2 If you end up with too narrow a gap along the wall in step 1, move over half the width of a tile by centering the middle tile over the vertical centerline.

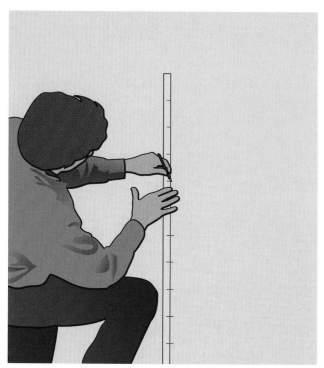

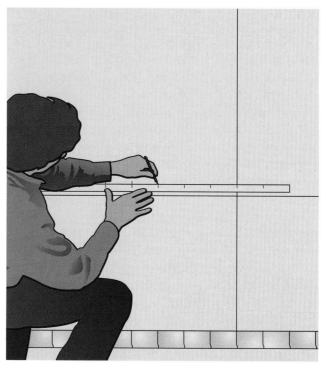

3 Use a story stick (see page 82) to determine whether your planned layout works vertically. If necessary, adjust the size of the first row of tile.

4 Dry-fit the first row of tile, then hold a story stick along the horizontal guideline with one grout line matched to the vertical reference line. Mark the grout lines, which will correspond with the grout lines of the first row and can be used as reference points.

Handling Outside Corners

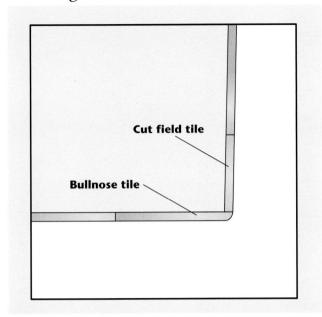

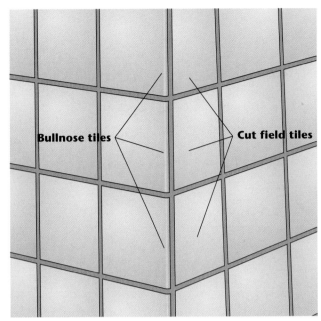

Overlap field tiles with bullnose tiles on outside corners. Try to use whole tiles on the corner, but if that's not possible, plan to trim the field tiles. If the wall is slightly out of plumb and not very wide, line up the bullnose tiles so they overlap the field tiles evenly.

Disguise walls that are badly out of plumb by installing the field tile on that side, trimming them as necessary. Overlap the cut edges with bullnose tiles. Install tiles on both walls at the same time, making sure the bullnose pieces cover the cut edges.

Laying Out Tile Around Windows & Other Obstacles

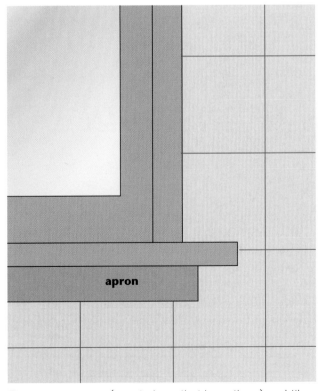

Use a story stick to evaluate the layout around obstacles, such as windows. Adjust reference lines as necessary to avoid cutting tiles by more than half, either vertically or horizontally.

Remove aprons (on windows that have them) and tile up to the window, then replace the trim. Aprons are the only window trim that can be removed and replaced in this manner.

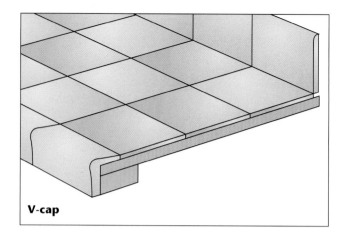

V-cap

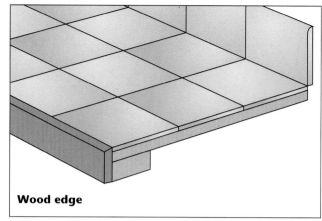

Wood edge

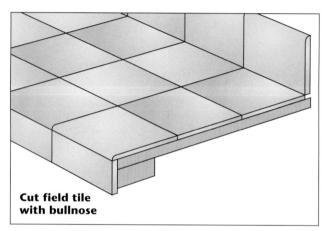

**Cut field tile
with bullnose**

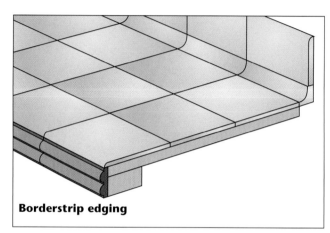

Borderstrip edging

Before you select tile, consider how you want to handle the backsplash and edging, and find out what trim pieces are available in the tile you want to use. You'll probably want to use a combination of field tile and edge tile, trim, or borders to create an attractive backsplash and edging.

Laying Out Countertop Projects

Y ou can lay tile over a laminate countertop that's square, level, and structurally sound. Use a belt sander with 60- or 80-grit sandpaper to rough up the surface before setting the tiles. If you're adding a new substrate and need to remove your existing countertop, remove all screws from beneath the countertop. If the countertop is secured with construction adhesive, cut the adhesive with a knife. Make sure the base cabinets are level front to back, side to side, and with adjoining cabinets. Unscrew a cabinet from the wall and use shims on the floor or against the wall to level it, if necessary.

Installing batten along the front edge of the countertop helps ensure the first row of tile is perfectly straight. For V-cap tiles, fasten a 1 × 2 batten along the reference line, using screws. The first row of field tile is placed against this

batten. For bullnose tiles, fasten a batten that's the same thickness as the edging tile, plus ⅛" for mortar thickness, to the face of the countertop so the top is flush with the top of the counter. The bullnose tiles are aligned with the outside edge of the batten. For wood edge trim, fasten a 1 × 2 batten to the face of the countertop so the top edge is above the top of the counter. The tiles are installed against the batten.

Before installing any tile, lay out the tiles in a dry run using spacers. If your counter is L-shaped, start at the corner and work outward. Otherwise, start the layout at a sink to ensure equal-sized cuts on both sides of the sink. If necessary, shift your starting point so you don't end up cutting very narrow tile segments.

Creating Starting Lines for Countertops

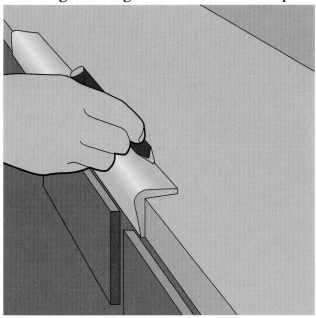

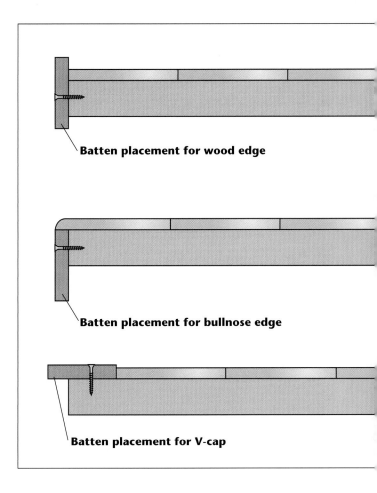

Batten placement for wood edge

Batten placement for bullnose edge

Batten placement for V-cap

1 If using V-cap tile, place it along the front edge of the substrate at one end of the countertop. Make a mark along the rear edge of the tile. Do the same at the opposite end of the countertop, then snap a chalk line between marks. Do this along the sides of the countertop as well.

2 Install battens along the edge of the countertop with screws to help line up the tile.

Installing Countertop Tile

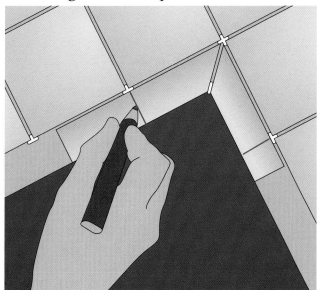

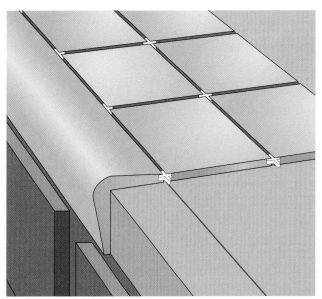

1 Lay out tiles and spacers in a dry run. Adjust starting lines, if necessary. Mix epoxy thin-set mortar and spread it with a ¼" square notched trowel. If using battens, lay the field tile flush with the battens, then apply edge tile. Otherwise, install the edging first. If the countertop has an inside corner, start there by installing a ready-made inside corner or cutting a 45° miter in edge tile to make your own inside corner.

2 Place the first row of field tile against the edge tile, separating the tile with spacers. Press the tiles gently in place without twisting them. Install remaining rows of tile the same way.

Getting Started

Purchasing Materials

Before you can select or purchase materials, you'll need to figure out exactly what you need and how much. Start by drawing a room layout, a reference for you and for anyone advising you about the project.

To estimate the amount of tile you need for a floor project, calculate the square footage of the room and add five percent for waste. For example, in a 10-foot × 12-foot room, the total area is 120 square feet. (12' × 10' = 120 sq. ft.). Add five percent, 6 square feet, for breakage and other waste (120 × .05 = 6 sq. ft.). You need to purchase enough tile to cover 126 square feet.

Tile cartons generally indicate the number of square feet one carton will cover. Divide the square footage to be covered by the square footage contained in a carton in order to determine the number of cartons required for your floor project. For example, if a carton holds 10 square feet, you will need 13 cartons to cover the 10 × 12 floor in our example.

Estimating tile for a wall project is slightly more complex. Start by deciding how much of each wall will be tiled. In a shower, plan to tile to at least 6" above the showerhead. It's common for tile to extend 4 feet up the remaining walls, although it's possible and sometimes very attractive for full walls to be tiled.

To calculate the amount of field tile required, measure each wall and multiply the width times the height of the area to be covered. Subtract the square footage of doors and windows. Do this for each wall, then add all the figures together to calculate the total square footage. Add five percent for waste. Calculate the number of cartons necessary (square footage of the project divided by the square footage contained in a carton).

Trim for floors and wall is sold by the lineal foot. Measure the lineal footage and calculate based on that. Plan carefully—the cost of trim tile adds up quickly. See pages 22 to 23 and 32 to 33 for further information on trim types and styles.

Before buying the tiles, ask about the dealer's return policy. Most dealers allow you to return unused tiles for a refund. In any case, think of it this way: buying a few too many tiles is a small problem. Running out of tiles when the job's almost done could turn into disaster if you can no longer get the tile or the colors don't match.

Estimating Tile Needs Example

Wall 1:	8 × 8 ft.	*64.00* sq. ft.
	– door 2.5 × 6.5	*16.25* sq. ft.
	=	47.75 sq. ft.
+ Wall 2:	8 × 10 ft.	80.00 sq. ft.
+ Wall 3:	8 × 8 ft.	*64.00* sq. ft.
	– window 2 × 4 ft.	*8.00* sq. ft.
	=	56.00 sq. ft.
+ Wall 4:	4 × 10 ft.	40.00 sq. ft.
Total wall coverage		223.75 sq. ft.
+ 5% waste		11.18 sq. ft.
New total tile needs		235.00 sq. ft.
÷ Amount of tile per carton (carton sizes vary)		10 sq. ft.
= Number of cartons needed		24 cartons

Use your room drawing to identify all the types of trim that will be necessary (above). Evaluate the trim available for the various tiles you're considering and select a combination that meets the specifications of your project.

Buy all necessary tile, tools, and materials at once to avoid wasted trips and to make sure all the elements are appropriate for one another and the project.

Design and paint your own custom tiles at many specialty ceramic stores. Order tile of the right size and have them bisque-fired but not glazed. You can then paint or stencil designs on the tile and have them fired. Look in the phone book for specialty ceramic stores.

Mix tile from carton to carton. Slight variations in color won't be as noticeable mixed throughout the project as they would be if the color shifts from one area to another.

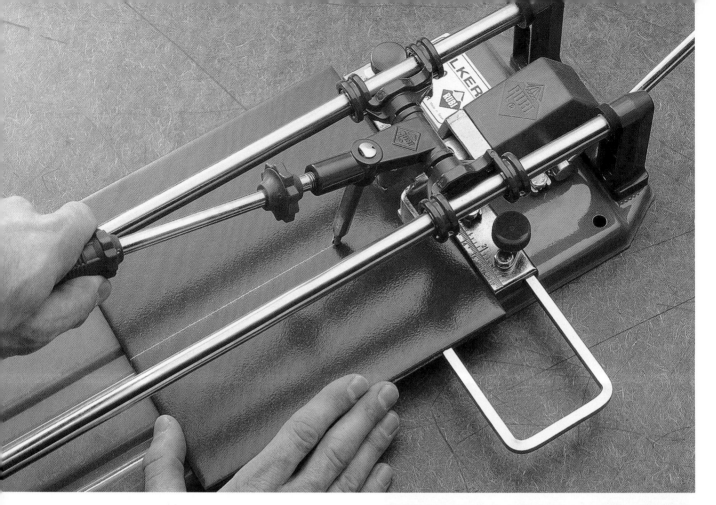

1 Mark a cutting line on the tile with a pencil, then place the tile in the cutter so the cutting wheel is directly over the line. While pressing down firmly on the wheel handle, run the wheel across the tile to score the surface. For a clean cut, score the tile only once.

2 Snap the tile along the scored line, as directed by the tool manufacturer. Usually, snapping the tile is accomplished by depressing a lever on the tile cutter.

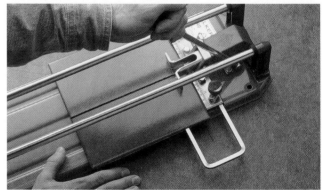

Cutting Tile

Careful planning will help you eliminate unnecessary cuts, but most tile jobs require cutting at least a few tiles and some jobs require cutting a large number of tiles, no matter how carefully you plan. For a few straight cuts on light- to medium-weight tile, use a snap cutter. If you're working with heavy tile or a large number of cuts on any kind of tile, a wet saw greatly simplifies the job. When using a wet saw, wear safety glasses and hearing protection. Make sure the blade is in good condition and the water container is full. Never use the saw without water, even for a few seconds.

Other cutting tools include nippers, hand-held tile cutters and rod saws. Nippers can be used on most types of tile, but a rod saw is most effective with wall tile, which generally is fairly soft.

A note of caution: hand-held tile cutters and tile nippers can create razor-sharp edges. Handle freshly cut tile carefully, and immediately round over the edges with a tile stone.

Before beginning a project, practice making straight and curved cuts on scrap tile.

Using a Wet Saw

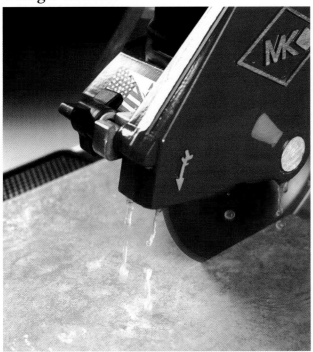

Individual saws vary so read the manufacturer's directions for use and make sure you understand them. Refer any questions to the rental center. Wear safety glasses and hearing protection; make sure water is reaching the blade at all times.

Place the tile on the sliding table and lock the fence to hold the tile in place, then press down on the tile as you slide it past the blade.

Marking Square Notches

1 Place the tile to be notched over the last full tile on one side of the corner. Set another full tile against the ½" spacer along the wall and trace along the opposite edge onto the second tile.

2 Move the top two tiles and spacer to the adjoining wall, making sure not to turn the tile that is being marked. Make a second mark on the tile as in step 1. Cut the tile and install.

Cutting Square Notches

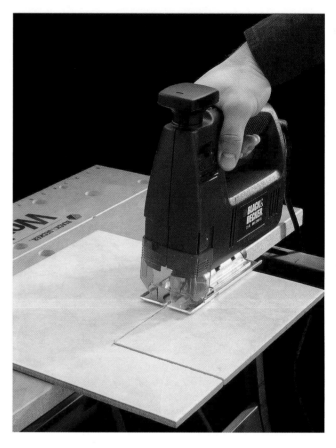

Cut along the marked line on one side of the notch. Turn the tile and cut along the other line to complete the notch. To keep the tile from breaking before you're through, slow down as you get close to the intersection with the first cut.

To cut square notches in a small number of wall tiles, clamp the tile down on a worktable, then use a jig saw with a tungsten carbide blade to make the cuts. If you need to notch quite a few tiles, a wet saw is more efficient.

To make a small number of cuts in wall tile, you can use a rod saw. Fit a tungsten carbide rod saw into a hacksaw body. Firmly support the tile and use a sawing motion to cut the tile.

To make a very small notch, use tile nippers. Score the lines and then nibble up to the lines, biting very small pieces at a time.

Marking & Cutting Irregular Notches

1 Make a paper template of the contour or use a contour gauge. To use a contour gauge, press the gauge onto the profile and trace it onto the tile.

2 Use a wet saw to make a series of closely spaced, parallel cuts, then nip away the waste.

Making Curved Cuts

1 Mark a cutting line on the tile face, then use the scoring wheel of a hand-held tile cutter to score the cut line. Make several parallel scores, no more than ¼" apart, in the waste portion of the tile.

2 Use tile nippers to nibble away the scored portion of the tile.

Marking & Cutting Holes in Tile

1 Align the tile to be cut with the last full row of tile and butt it against the pipe. Mark the center of the pipe onto the front edge of the tile.

2 Place a ¼" spacer against the wall and butt the tile against it. Mark the pipe center on the side edge of the tile. Using a combination square, draw a line through each mark to the edges of the tile.

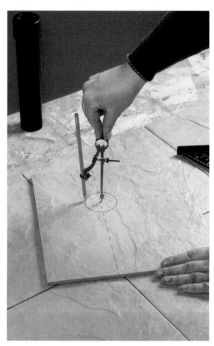

3 Starting from the intersection of the lines at the center, draw a circle slightly larger than the pipe or protrusion.

4 Drill around the edges of the hole, using a ceramic tile bit. Gently knock out the waste material with a hammer. The rough edges of the hole will be covered by a protective plate (called an escutcheon).

Variation: Score and cut the tile so the hole is divided in half, using the straight-cut method (page 98), then use the curved-cut method (page 101) to remove waste material from each half of the circle.

Drilling Holes in Tile

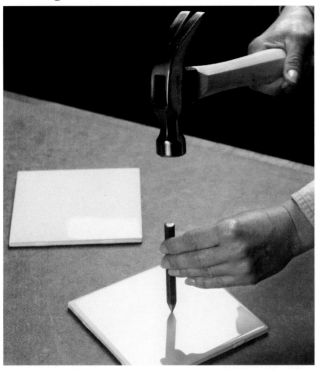

1 Make a dimple with a center punch to break through the glaze, to keep the drill bit from wandering.

2 Select a tungsten carbide hole saw in the appropriate size and attach it to a power drill. Place the tip at the marked center and drill the hole.

Making Specialty Cuts

Score cuts on mosaic tiles with a tile cutter in the row where the cut will occur. Cut away excess strips of mosaics from the sheet, using a utility knife, then use a handheld tile cutter to snap tiles one at a time.
Note: Use tile nippers to cut narrow portions of tiles after scoring.

103

To prepare small batches (above), add liquid, a little at a time, to the dry powder and stir the mixture until it has a creamy consistency. If you're adding liquid latex additive, mix it in when the mixture nears the proper consistency.

To prepare large batches or a series of batches (right), use a ½" drill and a mortar mixing paddle. This job easily can burn out a standard ⅜" drill, so it's worth the money to rent a heavy-duty drill if you don't have one.

Mixing & Using Mortar

Thin-set mortar is a fine-grained cement product used to adhere underlayment to the subfloor and to bond ceramic tile to underlayment. Some mortars include a latex additive in the dry mix, but with others, you'll need to add liquid latex additive as you prepare the mortar.

When mixing mortar, start with the dry powder and gradually add water, stirring the mixture to achieve a creamy consistency. You want the mortar wet enough for the tiles to stick, but not so wet that it's runny. Once the mortar is spread on the floor or wall, the ridges of the mortar should hold their shape.

Mortar is spread on the underlayment or substrate with a notched trowel. The edge of the trowel creates furrows in the mortar bed, then tile is placed on the mortar using a twisting motion.

As you install tiles, spread only as much mortar as you can use in 10 minutes. If the mortar sits too long, it will begin to harden and the tiles will not adhere to it. If it does begin to harden, scrape it up, throw it away, and spread new mortar.

Using Mortar with Floor Tile

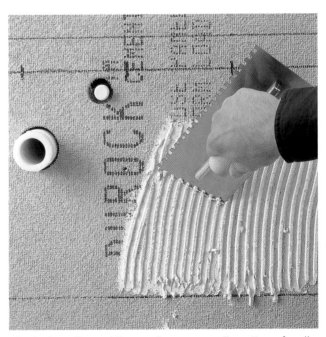

Spread mortar evenly onto the floor, using the appropriate trowel. Use the notched edge of the trowel to create furrows in the mortar bed.

Butter individual tiles by applying thin-set mortar directly to the back of the tile. Use the notched edge of the trowel to furrow the mortar.

Using Mortar with Wall Tile

Butter each wall tile and apply it to the wall with a slight twisting motion.

Variation: Spread the mortar on a small section of wall, then set the tiles into it. Thin-set mortar sets quickly, so work quickly if you choose this method.

105

Photo courtesy of Crossville Porcelain Stone

Floor Projects

Photo courtesy of Ceramic Tiles of Italy, opposite photo courtesy of Crossville Porcelain Stone

Photo courtesy of Ceramic Tiles of Italy

(*above*) In a large room, tile can be used to define functional spaces. In this contemporary living room, a conversation area is set apart by a border and change of setting pattern.

Let go of the notion that tile floors are reserved for kitchens and bathrooms. Tile lends style and distinction to all kinds of rooms.

(*above*) This tile floor provides a soothing, neutral setting for an artist's workspace.

(*opposite*) The tile floor and walls work with the furnishings to provide the illusion of a European villa in this suburban foyer.

Photo courtesy of Crossville Porcelain Stone

(*above*) With its black and white color scheme and diamond border, this tile floor is more than a match for its elegant setting.

Did you realize that simple squares and rectangles could be so decorative?

(*right*) Alternating taupe and white squares form an attractive border around this rustic sitting room.

(*far right*) Small squares set on the diagonal become diamonds to accent the corners of large square tiles.

Photo courtesy of Crossville Porcelain Stone

Photo courtesy of Ceramic Tiles of Italy

This photo and opposite photo courtesy of Crossville Porcelain Stone

(*above*) Within a mosaic border, rectangles in alternating colors are set to form an unusual but surprisingly uncomplicated pattern.

(*opposite*) This kitchen and eating area showcases a spectacular floor produced from black and cream squares and rectangles highlighted by golden squares set on the diagonal. An elaborate design like this requires very careful planning, but it's set using the same simple principles as any other floor.

(*above*) Spills happen, especially in kitchens. Polished stone makes an impressive kitchen floor, but only if the stone isn't slippery when wet. Porcelain with an impressed texture and non-slip glaze may be a better choice—it can provide the look without the hazard.

Durable, attractive, and easy to clean, tile is an excellent choice for kitchen floors.

(*above*) This stone floor mingles with stone countertops and stainless steel appliances in a kitchen fit for a true chef.

(*opposite*) Rectangular tiles flow with the long, lean lines of this galley kitchen, and their muted color sets the stage for the gleaming stainless steel accents.

(*above*) Variations in the setting pattern and a mosaic border around the center island provide touches of texture and color.

Photo courtesy of Crossville Porcelain Stone

Photo courtesy of Ikea Home Furnishings

Tile floors and bathrooms go together like peanut butter and jelly.

(*above left*) The shape and size of this luxurious bathroom is emphasized by the converging grout lines, which match the color of the paint in the room.

(*above right*) The multitude of grout lines makes mosaic tile naturally slip resistant, a wonderful quality for bathroom floors. The light, slightly uneven tones in this mosaic floor make the room seem larger than it is.

(*right*) The raised curb on this open shower keeps most of the water headed toward the drain. But no matter, the entire bathroom is tiled, so stray droplets are no problem.

(*opposite*) Combined with a huge window and vintage accents, quarry tile helps create the feeling that this bathroom is a natural extension of the porch beyond. Quarry tile should be sealed before being installed in locations that will be frequently exposed to water.

Photo courtesy of Ceramic Tiles of Italy

114

Installing Ceramic Floor Tile

EVERYTHING YOU NEED

Tools: chalk line, ¼" square-notched trowel, drill, rubber mallet, tile-cutting tools, needlenose pliers, utility knife, grout float, grout sponge, buff rag, foam brush.

Materials: tile, thin-set mortar, tile spacers, 2 × 4, threshold material, grout, latex additive (mortar and grout), grout sealer, silicone caulk.

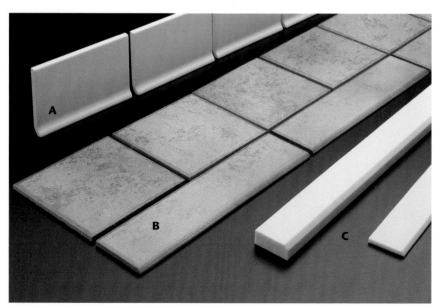

Trim and finishing materials for tile installations include base-trim tiles (A), which fit around the room perimeter, and bullnose tiles (B), used at doorways and other transition areas. Doorway thresholds (C) are made from synthetic materials as well as natural materials, such as marble, and come in thicknesses ranging from ¼" to ¾" to match different floor levels.

Tile flooring should be durable and slip-resistant. Look for floor tile that is textured or soft-glazed—for slip resistance—and has a Class or Group rating of 3, 4, or 5—for strength. Floor tile also should be glazed for protection from staining. If you use unglazed tile, be sure to seal it properly after installation. See pages 12 through 23 for more information on selecting floor tile.

Standard grouts also need stain protection. Mix your grout with a latex additive, and apply a grout sealer after the new grout sets, then reapply the sealer once a year thereafter.

Successful tile installation involves careful preparation of the floor and the proper combination of materials. For an underlayment, cementboard is the best for use over wood subfloors in bathrooms, since it is stable and undamaged by moisture (page 42). Thin-set is the most common adhesive for floor tile. It comes as a dry powder that is mixed with water. Pre-mixed organic adhesives generally are not recommended for floors.

If you want to install trim tiles, consider their placement as you plan the layout. Some base-trim tile is set on the floor, with its finished edge flush with the field tile; other types are installed on top of the field tile.

Overview: Installing Cementboard Underlayment

1 Starting at the longest wall, spread thin-set mortar on the subfloor in a figure-eight pattern. Spread only enough mortar for one sheet at a time. (See pages 104 to 105 for full description of mixing and applying thin-set mortar.) Set the cementboard on the mortar with the rough side up, making sure the edges are offset from the subfloor seams.

2 Fasten cementboard to the subfloor, using 1½" cementboard screws. Drive the screw heads flush with the surface. Continue spreading mortar and installing sheets along the wall, leaving a ⅛" gap at all joints and a ¼" gap along the room perimeter. (See page 62 for full description of installing cementboard.)

Overview: Establishing Reference Lines for Floor Tile Installation

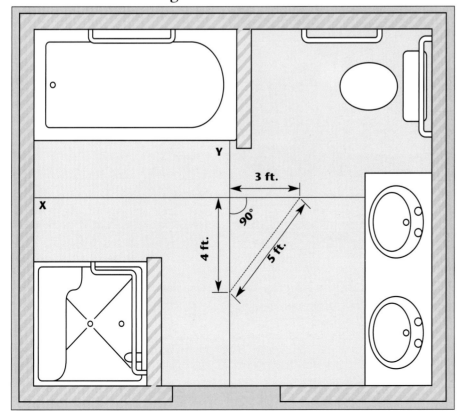

To establish reference lines, position the first line (X) between the centerpoints of opposite sides of the room. Snap a chalk line between these points.

Next, establish a second line perpendicular to the first. Snap a second reference line (Y) across the room.

Make sure the lines are exactly perpendicular, using the 3-4-5 triangle method. (For a full description of establishing perpendicular reference lines for floor projects, see page 83.)

Installing Ceramic Floor Tile

1 Draw reference lines and dry-fit full tiles along both lines, adjusting the layout as necessary. Mix a batch of thin-set mortar (see pages 104 to 105), and spread it evenly against both reference lines of one quadrant. Use the notched edge of the trowel to create furrows in the mortar bed. *Note:* For large or uneven tiles, you may need a trowel with ⅜" or larger notches.

2 Set the first tile in the corner of the quadrant where the reference lines intersect. When setting tiles that are 8" square or larger, twist each tile slightly as you set it into position. (If using stone tile, see pages 122 to 123 for information on preparing the tile.)

3 Using a soft rubber mallet, gently rap the central area of each tile a few times to set it evenly into the mortar.

Variation: For mosaic sheets, use a ³⁄₁₆" V-notched trowel to spread the mortar, and use a grout float to press the sheets into the mortar. Apply pressure gently to avoid creating an uneven surface.

4 To ensure consistent spacing between tiles, place plastic tile spacers at the corners of the set tile. *Note:* With mosaic sheets, use spacers equal to the gaps between tiles.

5 Set tiles into the mortar along the reference lines. Make sure the tiles fit neatly against the spacers. To make sure the tiles are level with one another, lay a straight piece of 2 × 4 across several tiles, and rap the board with a mallet. Lay tile in the remaining area covered with mortar. Repeat steps 1 through 5, working in small sections, until you reach walls or fixtures.

6 Measure and mark tiles for cutting to fit against walls and into corners, then cut the tiles to fit, following the tips on pages 98 to 103. Apply thin-set mortar directly to the back of the cut tiles, instead of the floor, using the notched edge of the trowel to furrow the mortar. Set the tiles.

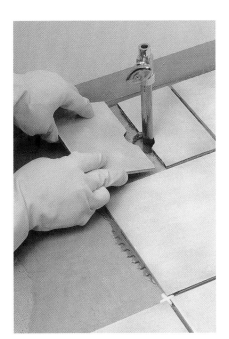

7 Measure, cut, and install tiles requiring notches or curves to fit around obstacles, such as exposed pipes or toilet drains.

8 Remove the spacers with needlenose pliers before the mortar hardens. Inspect the joints and remove high spots of mortar that could show through the grout, using a utility knife. Install tile in the remaining quadrants, completing one quadrant at a time.

9 Install threshold material in doorways. Set the threshold in thin-set mortar so the top is even with the tile. Use the same spacing used for the tiles. Let the mortar cure for at least 24 hours.

(continued next page)

10 Mix a small batch of grout, following the manufacturer's directions. (For unglazed or stone tile, add a release agent to prevent the grout from bonding to the tile surfaces.) Starting in a corner, pour the grout over the tile. Spread the grout outward from the corner, pressing firmly on the grout float to completely fill the joints. For best results, tilt the float at a 60° angle to the floor and use a figure-eight motion.

11 Use the grout float to remove excess grout from the surface of the tile. Wipe diagonally across the joints, holding the float in a nearly vertical position. Continue applying grout and wiping off excess until about 25 sq. ft. of the floor has been grouted.

12 Remove excess grout by wiping a damp grout sponge diagonally over about 2 sq. ft. of the tile at a time. Rinse the sponge in cool water between wipes. Wipe each area only once; repeated wiping can pull grout from the joints. Repeat steps 10 through 12 to apply grout to the rest of the floor. Allow the grout to dry for about 4 hours, then use a soft cloth to buff the tile surface and remove any remaining grout film.

13 After the grout has cured completely (check the manufacturer's instructions), apply grout sealer to the grout lines, using a small sponge brush or sash brush. Avoid brushing sealer onto the tile surfaces. Wipe up any excess sealer immediately.

Installing Base & Trim Tile

1 Dry-fit the trim tiles to determine the best spacing (grout lines in base tile do not always align with grout lines in the floor tile). Use rounded bullnose tiles at outside corners, and mark tiles for cutting as needed.

2 Leaving a ⅛" expansion gap between tiles at corners, mark any contour cuts necessary to allow the coved edges to fit together. Use a jig saw with a tungsten carbide blade to make curved cuts.

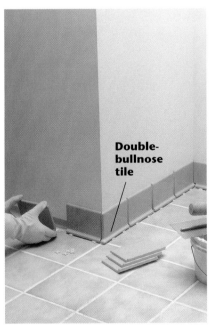

Double-bullnose tile

3 Begin installing base-trim tiles at an inside corner. Use a notched trowel to apply wall-tile adhesive to the back of each tile. Slip ⅛" spacers under the tiles to create an expansion joint. Set the tiles by pressing them firmly onto the wall.

4 At outside corners, use a double-bullnose tile on one side to cover the edge of the adjoining tile.

5 After the adhesive dries, grout the vertical joints between tiles, and apply grout along the tops of the tiles to make a continuous grout line. After the grout cures, fill the expansion joint at the bottom of the tiles with silicone caulk.

Setting a Running Bond Tile Pattern

1 Start running bond tile by dry-fitting tile to establish working reference lines. Dry-fit a few tiles side by side using spacers. Measure the total width of the fitted section (A). Use this measurement to snap a series of equally spaced parallel lines to help keep your tiles straight during installation.

2 Starting at a point where the layout lines intersect, spread thin-set mortar to a small section and lay the first row of tiles. Apply mortar directly to the underside of any tiles that extend outside the mortar bed. Offset the next row by a measurement that's equal to one-half the length of the tile and one-half the width of the grout line.

3 Continue setting tiles, filling one quadrant at a time. Use the parallel reference lines as guides to keep the rows straight. Immediately wipe away any mortar from the surface of the tiles. When finished, allow the mortar to cure, then grout and clean the tile (see pages 154 to 156).

Setting Hexagonal Tile

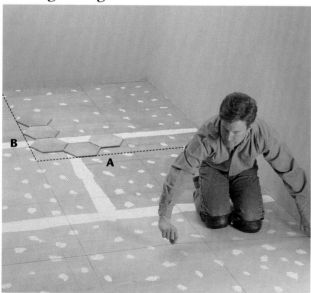

1 Snap perpendicular reference lines on the underlayment. Lay out three or four tiles in each direction along the layout lines. Place plastic spacers between the tiles to maintain even spacing. Measure the length of this layout in both directions (A and B). Use measurement A to snap a series of equally spaced parallel lines across the entire floor, then do the same for measurement B in the other direction.

2 Apply thin-set mortar to small sections at a time and begin setting tile. Apply mortar directly to the underside of any tiles that extend outside the mortar bed. Continue setting the tiles, using the grid layout and spacers to keep the tiles aligned. Wipe off any mortar from the tile surface. When finished, allow the mortar to set, then grout.

Setting a Diagonal Pattern within a Border

1 Plan your border layout in the room (see pages 85 to 86). Dry-fit border tiles with spacers in the planned area. Make sure the border tiles are aligned with the reference lines. Dry-fit tiles at the outside corners of the border arrangement. Adjust the tile positions as necessary to create a layout with minimal cutting. When the layout of the tiles is set, snap chalk lines around the border tiles and trace along the edges of the outside tiles. Install the border tiles.

2 Draw diagonal layout lines at a 45° angle to the perpendicular reference lines.

3 Use standard tile-setting techniques to set field tiles inside the border. Kneel on a wide board to distribute your weight if you need to work in a tiled area that has not cured overnight.

Setting a Stone & Mosaic Tile Floor

The project that follows combines 4 × 4" tumbled stone with a stone mosaic medallion and border to produce a decorative effect in an entryway. This idea could be adapted for many rooms. You could border a seating area or create the effect of a rug in front of a fireplace, for example. To lay out a similar design, refer to pages 85 and 86, then center the medallion within the border.

The techniques for setting natural stone are virtually the same ones used with ceramic tile. There are several special considerations, however.

First, stone tile cracks more easily than ceramic. It's extremely important to provide a firm, flat substrate for stone tile projects, especially when you're using large tiles. The larger the tile, the more susceptible it is to stress fractures if the floor structure doesn't support it adequately. See pages 56 to 58 for more information on repairing and strengthening subfloors; see pages 60 to 62 for information on installing underlayment.

Natural stone is subject to greater variation from one tile to the next than manufactured materials. Cartons of some stone tile, especially larger polished stone varieties, may include warped tiles. Be sure to buy enough tile that any severely warped tiles can be sorted out and returned.

Some stone should be sealed before it's set because grout tends to stain it. Ask your dealer for specific recommendations.

EVERYTHING YOU NEED

Tools: chalk line, ¼" square-notched trowel, rubber mallet, tile-cutting tools, needlenose pliers, utility knife, grout float, grout sponge, buff rag, foam brush.

Materials: 4 × 4" stone tile, mosaic tile, mosaic medallion, thin-set mortar, tile spacers, 2 × 4 lumber, threshold material, grout, latex additive (mortar and grout), grout sealer, silicone caulk.

Tips for Setting Stone Tile Floors

Check for warped tiles. Lay polished stone tiles next to one another and check carefully. Mark tiles that are slightly warped and build up thinset mortar to level them during installation. Return significantly warped tile to the dealer.

Make sure the subfloor is flat and firm. If problems exist, resolve them before beginning the tile project (see pages 56 to 58). This is important for any stone tile floor but critical for a polished stone tile floor.

Dry-lay polished stone tile floors, with 1/16" spacers. (Plan to use unsanded grout.) Use larger spacers (and sanded grout) for informal stone floors.

Use white thin-set mortar for light-colored marble, travertine, and other natural stones, which are somewhat translucent. Take extra care to create a very even surface when combing the mortar.

Seal tiles before installation to help keep contrasting grout from staining the stone. Check manufacturer's recommendations or consult your tile retailer for suggestions. This is particularly important when dealing with porous or rough-surfaced stone.

Keep grout from staining stone tile by wiping the tiles early and often, using a clean, damp cloth.

1 Measure the area and make a scaled diagram of the space. Measure the mosaic medallion and determine the size and placement of the bordered area (see pages 80 through 86 for details).

2 Install and tape cementboard in the project area. (See pages 60 to 63 for full details.)

3 Snap perpendicular reference lines. Check the lines for squareness, using the "3-4-5 triangle" method (see pages 82 to 83 for further information).

4 On each line, mark a point equally distant from the center. If your mosaic medallion is a 12" square, mark the points at 12"; if it's a 24" square, mark the points at 24", and so on. Snap chalk lines to connect the points, establishing lines at a 45° angle.

5 Following the layout created in step 1, measure and mark placement lines for the border. (Make sure these lines are aligned with the first set of reference lines.) Cut mosaic tiles into strips and dry-fit the border.

6 Dry-fit the tiles at the outside corners of the border arrangement, aligning the tile with the diagonal reference lines. Use spacers and adjust as necessary. When the layout of the tiles is set, trace the edges of the outside tiles.

7 Set the field tile, cutting tile as necessary (see pages 118 to 121 for full details on setting tile). Remove the spacers. Let the mortar cure according to manufacturer's instructions. Set the border tile.

8 Place the medallion in the center of the bordered area, aligning it with the diagonal reference lines. Dry-fit the field tiles within the border, using spacers and aligning the tile with the perpendicular reference lines.

(continued next page)

9 For tricky cuts, make paper templates to match the tile size. Later, use the templates to mark tiles for cutting.

10 Determine placement of accent tiles within field tile. Measure the field accent tile and mark cutting lines on field tile to accommodate them.

11 Set medallion, then the field tile within the border. (Again, avoid placing your weight on newly set tiles.) Remove the spacers and let the mortar dry overnight or according to manufacturer's instructions.

Tip: If absolutely necessary to work from newly set tile, kneel on a wide board to distribute your weight.

12 Install threshold material in doorways. Set the threshold in thin-set mortar so the top is even with the tile. Use the same spacing used for the tiles. Let the mortar cure for at least 24 hours.

13 Prepare a small batch of grout and fill the tile joints (see page 120 for details on grouting tile). When the grout has cured, seal the grout lines, using a small sponge brush or sash brush.

14 Add wood baseboards or base-trim tiles at the edges of the room.

Creating & Setting a Floor Mosaic

As an art form, mosaic has been around for centuries. In fact, the oldest known mosaic floor, found in Turkey, dates to approximately 700 B.C. Although mosaic truly is an art form, its use isn't restricted to artisans. Pre-made mosaics set on mesh are widely available, and with modern materials anyone with the time and patience can produce an original mosaic.

Until recently, making intricate mosaics required quite a bit of both time and patience, but recent innovations have changed all that for anyone who prefers a more streamlined approach. Computer programs can now read

EVERYTHING YOU NEED

Tools: chalk line, ¼" square-notched trowel, rubber mallet, tile-cutting tools, needlenose pliers, utility knife, grout float, grout sponge, buff rag, foam brush.

Materials: software program for mosaic design, mosaic floor tile, mosaic mounting media, tile grids, photograph or other image, floor tile, thin-set mortar, tile spacers, grout, latex additive (mortar and grout), grout sealer.

an image file, assign tile colors to it, and create a pattern. Some programs even produce a shopping list for the project. As you might imagine, this greatly simplifies and speeds up the process.

For the project shown here, we used TileCreator software, tile grids, and Mosaic Mount mounting media, all available through retailers that carry mosaic supplies, as well as through a growing number of on-line suppliers (see Resources, page 246, for further details). The program produces a shopping list and a pattern in a paint-by-numbers type of chart that's amazingly easy to follow.

The program also includes step-by-step instructions that lead you through creating a pattern, but we've included a general description here to give you an idea of what's required. You do need to know how to use a computer and import files into the program, but you don't need to be a technical genius to make it work.

We used 1" tiles for the mosaic, but ¾" work as well. Refer to pages 80 through 86 for information on laying out the floor.

Choosing a Mosaic Image

1 Look through family photographs, magazines, postcards, and catalogs for images. (Always be aware and respectful of copyright laws.) Scan several images at 72 to 150 dpi. If you don't have access to a scanner, have the images scanned at a copy center. Save the images as JPG, BMP, or TIF files.

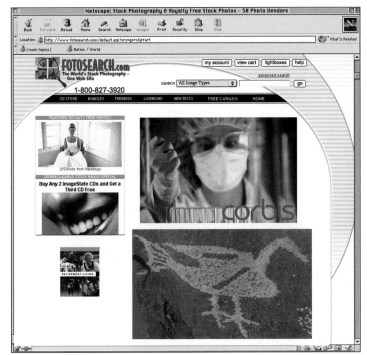

2 Download images from clip art CDs or the Internet. (Look for images with distinct shapes and colors.) Again, 72 to 150 dpi works best. Save the images as JPG, BMP, or TIF files.

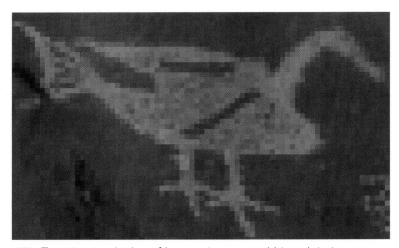

3 To get a rough idea of how an image would translate to a mosaic, reduce the number of pixels until the image has a graph paper look.

Using TileCreator® Software

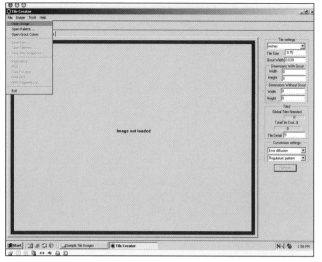

1 Import an image into the program. (The image should be no larger than 5 megabytes, no more than 300 dpi in resolution, and use RGB colors.)

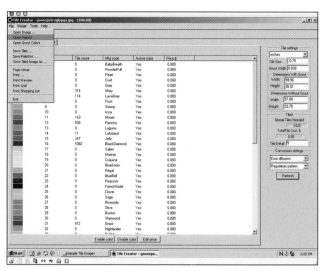

2 Review the color palettes to see which offers more of the main colors included in the image. Select one color palette.

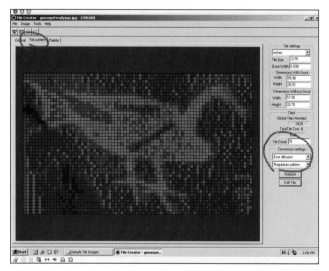

3 Experiment with the settings for the grout width, image dimensions, and color conversion. Try both tile patterns—regulatum (straight rows and columns) and tessulatum (offset columns). Note the final dimensions of the mosaic.

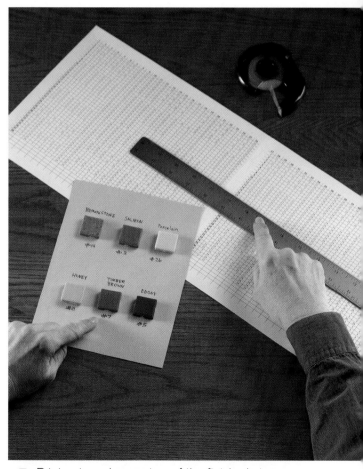

4 Print out a color preview of the finished piece, a shopping list of the colors required, and a numbered chart corresponding to the tile colors of the shopping list.

Laying Out the Floor

1 Prepare the subfloor and underlayment in the project area, then establish reference lines. (See pages 46 to 77 for information on preparing the project area.)

2 Create a layout and determine placement of the mosaic (see pages 80 to 86 for details). Snap lines to mark the mosaic area, then dry-fit the field tile around that area.

3 Set the field tile in thin-set mortar and let it dry thoroughly. (See pages 118 to 121 for more information on setting tile.)

4 Measure the tile grids (see page 132) and mark corresponding quadrants onto the mosaic area.

Creating the Mosaic

1 Identify each tile color by number. Following the numbered chart generated through the software, assemble the tile in the grids. Work in sections corresponding to one grid frame at a time and mark off each row as it's completed.

2 As each frame is completed, cover it with mosaic mounting media. Peel the backing off the media and gradually press it down over the tile grid. Burnish the media to make sure it's adhered to each tile.

3 Grasp the mosaic media at the corners and lift the tile from the grid. (These sections of the mosaic are surprisingly stable, but handle them with care to make sure the tiles stay in place.)

4 One quadrant at a time, spread thin-set mortar on the underlayment and position the mosaic. Use a grout float to seat the tile in the mortar. (See pages 118 to 121 for more information on setting tile.)

5 When the mortar is thoroughly dry, carefully peel the mosaic media away from the set tiles.

6 Spread grout over the tile and press it into the joints using a grout float. Wipe away excess grout with a sponge, then polish off any residue. (See page 120 for further information on grouting tile.)

Variation: Converting Cross-stitch Patterns to Mosaic Tile Images

1 If you don't have access to the necessary computer equipment to create your own mosaic patterns, try using a cross-stitch pattern. Enlarge a pattern on a copier and determine a portion of the pattern to be used and the size of the mosaic.

2 Select tile and assign tile colors to the various colors of thread as indicated. Follow the pattern to set the tile in the tile grids. Complete the floor as described in the preceding pages.

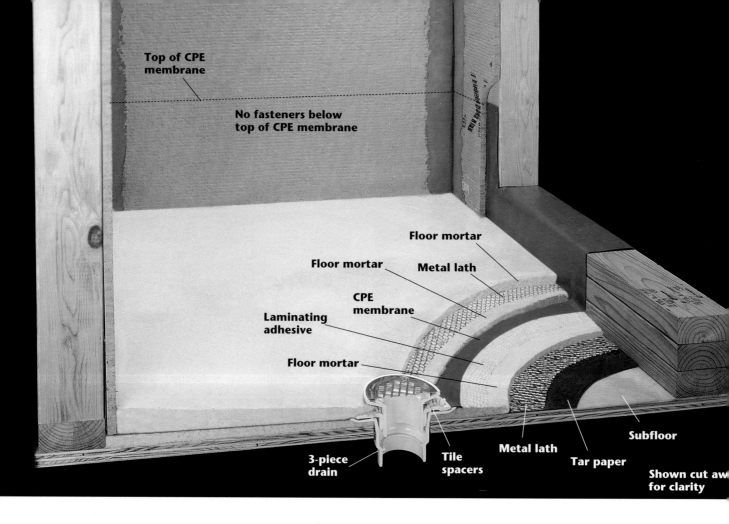

Top of CPE membrane

No fasteners below top of CPE membrane

Floor mortar

Floor mortar

Metal lath

CPE membrane

Laminating adhesive

Floor mortar

3-piece drain

Tile spacers

Metal lath

Tar paper

Subfloor

Shown cut aw for clarity

Building a Custom-tiled Shower Base

A custom-tiled shower base offers you great flexibility in the location and size of your shower. Building the base is quite simple, though it does require time and some knowledge of basic masonry techniques because the base is formed primarily using mortar.

EVERYTHING YOU NEED

Tools: tape measure, circular saw, hammer, utility knife, stapler, 2-ft. level, mortar mixing box, trowel, wood float, felt-tip marker, ratchet wrench, expandable stopper, drill, tin snips, torpedo level, tools for installing tile (pages 40 to 41).

Materials: 2 × 4 and 2 × 10 framing lumber, 16d galvanized common nails, 15# building paper, staples, 3-piece shower drain, PVC primer, PVC cement, galvanized finish nails, galvanized metal lath, thick-bed floor mortar ("deck mud"), latex mortar additive, laminating adhesive, CPE waterproof membrane & preformed dam corners, CPE membrane solvent glue, CPE membrane sealant, cementboard and materials for installing cementboard (page 42), materials for installing tile (page 43).

A custom-tiled shower base is built in three layers to ensure proper water drainage: the pre pan, the shower pan, and the shower floor. A mortar pre pan is first built on top of the subfloor, establishing a slope toward the drain of ¼" for every 12" of shower floor. Next, a waterproof chlorinated polyethylene (CPE) membrane forms the shower pan, providing a watertight seal for the shower base. Finally, a second mortar bed reinforced with wire mesh is installed for the shower floor, providing a surface for tile installation. If water penetrates the tiled shower floor, the shower pan and sloped pre pan will direct it to the weep holes of the 3-piece drain.

One of the most important steps in building a custom-tiled shower base is testing the shower pan after installation (step 13). This allows you to locate and fix any leaks to prevent costly damage.

The materials needed to build this shower base can be found at most home centers or at tile specialty stores. Be sure to contact your local building department regarding code restrictions and to secure the necessary permits.

Curb

1 Remove building materials to expose subfloor and stud walls (see pages 46 through 71). Cut three 2 × 4s for the curb and fasten them to the floor joists and the studs at the shower threshold with 16d galvanized common nails. Also cut 2 × 10 lumber to size and install in the stud bays around the perimeter of the shower base.

2 Staple 15# building paper to the subfloor of the shower base. Disassemble the 3-piece shower drain and glue the bottom piece to the drain pipe with PVC cement. Partially screw the drain bolts into the drain piece, and stuff a rag into the drain pipe to prevent mortar from falling into the drain.

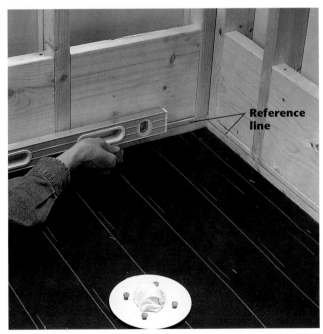

Reference line

3 Mark the height of the bottom drain piece on the wall farthest from the center of the drain. Measure from the center of the drain straight across to that wall, then raise the height mark ¼" for every 12" of shower floor to slope the pre pan toward the drain. Trace a reference line at the height mark around the perimeter of the entire alcove, using a level.

Metal lath

4 Staple galvanized metal lath over the building paper; cut a hole in the lath ½" from the drain. Mix floor mortar (or "deck mud") to a fairly dry consistency, using a latex additive for strength; mortar should hold its shape when squeezed (inset). Trowel the mortar onto the subfloor, building the pre pan from the flange of the drain piece to the height line on the perimeter of the walls.

(continued next page)

Building a Custom-tiled Shower Base, continued

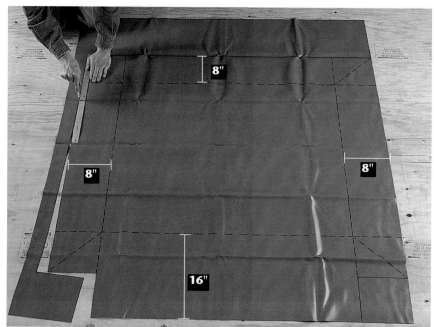

5 Continue using the trowel to form the pre pan, checking the slope using a level and filling any low spots with mortar. Finish the surface of the pre pan with a wood float until it is even and smooth. Allow the mortar to cure overnight.

6 Measure the dimensions of the shower floor, and mark it out on a sheet of CPE waterproof membrane, using a felt-tipped marker. From the floor outline, measure out and mark an additional 8" for each wall and 16" for the curb end. Cut the membrane to size, using a utility knife and straightedge. Be careful to cut on a clean, smooth surface to prevent puncturing the membrane.

7 Measure to find the exact location of the drain and mark it on the membrane, outlining the outer diameter of the drain flange. Cut a circular piece of CPE membrane roughly 2" larger than the drain flange, then use CPE membrane solvent glue to weld it into place and reinforce the seal at the drain.

8 Coat the pre pan, curb, and perimeter blocking with laminating adhesive and a notched trowel, then apply CPE sealant around the drain. Fold the membrane along the floor outline. Set the membrane over the pre pan so the reinforced drain seal is centered over the drain bolts.

9 Working from the drain to the walls, carefully smooth out any bubbles from under the membrane. Tuck the membrane tight into each corner, folding the extra material into triangular flaps. Apply CPE solvent glue to one side, press the flap flat, then staple it in place (inset). Staple only the top edge of the membrane to the blocking; do not staple below the top of the curb, or on the curb itself.

10 At the shower curb, cut the membrane along the studs so it can be folded over the curb. Solvent-glue a dam corner at each inside corner of the curb. Do not fasten the dam corners with staples.

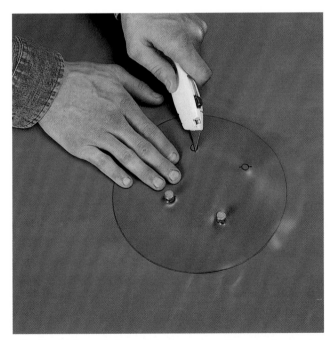

11 At the reinforced drain seal on the membrane, locate and mark the drain bolts. Press the membrane down around the bolts, then use a utility knife to carefully cut a slit just large enough for the bolts to poke through. Push the membrane down over the bolts.

12 Use a utility knife to carefully cut away only enough of the membrane to expose the drain and allow the middle drain piece to fit in place. Remove the drain bolts, then position the middle drain piece over the bolt holes. Reinstall the bolts, tightening them evenly and firmly to create a watertight seal.

(continued next page)

Building a Custom-tiled Shower Base, continued

13 Test the shower pan for leaks overnight. Place a balloon tester (inset) in the drain below the weep holes, and fill the pan with water, to 1" below the top of the curb. Mark the water level and let the water sit overnight. If the water level remains the same, the pan holds water. If the level is lower, locate and fix leaks in the pan using patches of membrane and CPE solvent.

14 Install cementboard on the alcove walls (pages 74 to 75), using ¼" wood shims to lift the bottom edge off the CPE membrane. To prevent puncturing the membrane, do not use fasteners in the lower 8" of the cementboard. Cut a piece of metal lath to fit around the three sides of the curb. Bend the lath so it tightly conforms to the curb. Pressing the lath against the top of the curb, staple it to the outside face of the curb. Mix enough mortar for the two sides of the curb.

15 Overhang the front edge of the curb with a straight 1× board, so it is flush with the outer wall material. Apply mortar to the mesh with a trowel, building to the edge of the board. Clear away excess mortar, then use a torpedo level to check for plumb, making adjustments as needed. Repeat for the inside face of the curb. *Note:* The top of the curb will be finished after tile is installed (step 19). Allow the mortar to cure overnight.

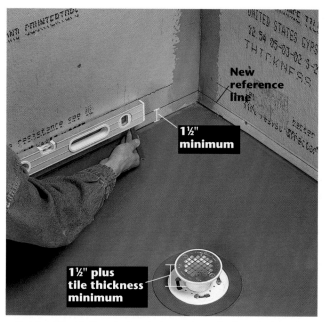

16 Attach the drain strainer piece to the drain, adjusting it to a minimum of 1½" above the shower pan. On one wall, mark 1½" up from the shower pan, then use a level to draw a reference line around the perimeter of the shower base. Because the pre pan establishes the ¼" per foot slope, this measurement will maintain that slope.

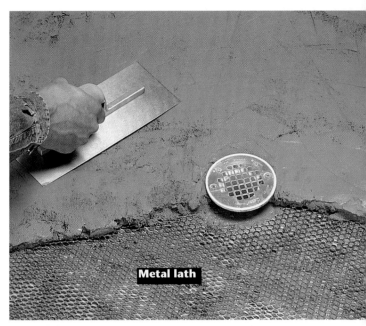

Metal lath

17 Spread tile spacers over the weep holes of the drain to prevent mortar from plugging the holes. Mix the floor mortar, then build up the shower floor to roughly half the thickness of the base. Cut metal lath to cover the mortar bed, keeping it ½" from the drain (see photo in step 18).

18 Continue to add mortar, building the floor to the reference line on the walls. Use a level to check the slope, and pack mortar into low spots with a trowel. Leave space at the drain for the thickness of the tile. Float the surface using a wood float until it is smooth and slopes evenly to the drain. When finished, allow the mortar to cure overnight before installing the tiles.

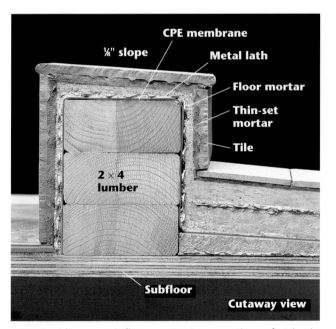

CPE membrane

⅛" slope

Metal lath

Floor mortar

Thin-set mortar

Tile

2 × 4 lumber

Subfloor

Cutaway view

19 After the floor has cured, draw reference lines and establish the tile layout, then mix a batch of thin-set mortar and install the floor tile (pages 118 to 121). At the curb, cut the tiles for the inside to protrude ½" above the unfinished top of the curb, and the tiles for the outside to protrude ⅝" above the top, establishing a ⅛" slope so water drains back into the shower. Use a level to check the tops of the tiles for level as you work.

20 Mix enough floor mortar to cover the unfinished top of the curb, then pack it in place between the tiles, using a trowel. Screed off the excess mortar flush with the tops of the side tiles. Allow the mortar to cure, then install bullnose cap tile. Install the wall tile, then grout, clean, and seal all the tile (pages 154 to 157). After the grout has cured fully, run a bead of silicone caulk around all inside corners to create control joints.

Photo courtesy of Walker Zanger, Inc.

Wall Projects

(*above*) Handpainted tiles set together make a striking statement on an otherwise plain wall.

Combining different colors and types of tile often produces interesting, appealing walls.

(*above*) Simple square tile takes on new personality when topped by a mosaic border set off with liners.

(*opposite*) Strategically placed decorative tile within a field of plainer, less expensive tile generates lots of interest at a reasonable price. Adding borders in similar colors further emphasizes the decorative tile.

(*right*) They require careful planning, but stunning effects can be achieved through color banding and variations in setting patterns. On the wall at the far right in this bathroom, border tile and liners sparkle against white tile. On the wall at left, liners frame the mirror, which is set within a frame of white and decorative tile. Framed by liners and a diagonal set, the sink becomes a decorative element for the room.

Interesting setting patterns create appealing rooms.

(*right*) Mitering the corners adds special interest to ledges and countertops.

(*far right*) Called subway tile, tiles in this size and shape are often set with the joints offset rather than aligned. This attractive pattern isn't difficult, but does require more careful planning than a traditional set.

This photo and opposite photo courtesy of Ceramic Tiles of Italy

These photos illustrate clever strategies that also can be put to use in smaller, simpler rooms.

(*above*) This large contemporary bathroom is broken into distinct functional areas by the tile. The doorless shower is defined by field tile in a straight set, while the dressing area is marked by a border and the reversal of color between the field and the edges. The mirror above the sink is framed by field tile set on the diagonal. Finally, the sink area is set off by a shift in the size and shape of the field tile.

(*opposite*) Although the wall is set with a combination of similar tiles, liners and listellos mark the transition from a straight to a diagonal set. This breaks up what would otherwise be a broad—and possibly boring—expanse of plain tile.

Tiling walls visually ties them to tiled floors and countertops.

(*above*) This mantel and fireplace surround rely on shape and size for effect, subtly blending into the floor without stealing too much attention from its distinctive pattern.

(*below*) A border of decorative tile, liners, and listellos wraps around a bench and frames the vanity with equal flair.

(*opposite*) Tile defines a hearth area and fireplace surround, and merges them into this tranquil setting.

149

Tile backsplashes are functional in addition to being beautiful.

(*above*) This contrasting backsplash and coordinated edging make a lovely counterpoint for the white cabinets, tile countertop, and apron sink.

Photo courtesy of Crossville Porcelain Stone

Photo courtesy of Fireclay Tile, Inc.

Photo courtesy of Ceramic Tiles of Italy

(*above center*) This backsplash protects the wall above the sink, which otherwise would be constantly exposed to water from the wall-mounted faucets. These handmade tiles are perfectly suited to this rustic setting.

(*above right*) Around sinks, tile backsplashes protect walls from water and food spills; around ranges, they protect walls from grease and smoke, too.

(*lower right*) Tile backsplashes are easy to clean, which is great when one of those inevitable kitchen mishaps occurs. Here, the color from the countertops extends up the walls, forming an eye-catching color band for the backsplash.

151

With thousands of types
and styles available, you
can find tile for virtually
any effect you could hope
to achieve.

(*above*) This border and the coordinated decorative tiles come
together in a backsplash that
complements the vintage style
of this homey kitchen.

(*right*) If borders appeal to you,
you'll find motifs to suit every
room of the house. This black-
berry vine is particularly well
suited to a kitchen.

(*above*) Tumbled or faux-stone tile produces a clean, neutral background in contemporary homes. Here the tiles sparkle amidst a subtle lighting scheme.

(*left*) Natural stone tile looks great in homes decorated around natural themes such as gardening.

(*lower left*) This crisp combination of blue and white tile is pulled straight from the floral floor tile. Together they create a wonderful setting for the room's Scandinavian-style furnishings.

Installing a Tile Wall

Tile is an ideal covering for walls in kitchens and bathrooms, but there's no reason to limit its use to those rooms. It's not as common in North American homes, but in Europe tile has been used in rooms throughout the house for generations. And why not? Beautiful, practical, easy to clean and maintain, tile walls are well suited to many spaces. On the preceding pages, you've seen some design ideas for tile walls. Now it's time to get down to business.

When shopping for tile, keep in mind that tiles that are at least 6" × 6" are easier to install than small tiles, because they require less cutting and cover more surface area.

EVERYTHING YOU NEED

Tools: tile-cutting tools, marker, tape measure, 4-ft. level, notched trowel, mallet, grout float, sponge, small paintbrush, caulk gun.

Materials: straight 1 × 2, dry-set tile mortar with latex additive, ceramic wall tile, ceramic trim tile (as needed), 2 × 4, carpet scrap, tile grout with latex additive, tub & tile caulk, alkaline grout sealer, cardboard.

Larger tiles also have fewer grout lines that must be cleaned and maintained. Check out the selection of trim and specialty tiles and ceramic accessories that are available to help you customize your project. (See pages 24 to 33 for information on selecting wall tile.)

Most wall tile is designed to have narrow grout lines (less than ⅛" wide) filled with unsanded grout. Grout lines wider than ⅛" should be filled with sanded floor-tile grout. Either type will last longer if it contains, or is mixed with, a latex additive. To prevent staining, it's a good idea to seal your grout after it fully cures, then once a year thereafter.

You can use standard drywall or water-resistant drywall (called "greenboard") as a backer for walls in dry areas. In wet areas, install tile over cementboard. Made from cement and fiberglass, cementboard cannot be damaged by water, though moisture can pass through it. To protect the framing, install a waterproof membrane, such as roofing felt or polyethylene sheeting, between the framing members and the cementboard. Be sure to tape and finish the seams between cementboard panels before laying the tile.

See pages 87 to 91 for information on planning and laying out tile walls.

1 Design the layout and mark the reference lines (see pages 87 to 91). Begin installation with the second row of tiles above the floor. If the layout requires cut tiles for this row, mark and cut the tiles for the entire row at one time.

2 Mix a small batch of thin-set mortar containing a latex additive. (Some mortar has additive mixed in by the manufacturer and some must have additive mixed in separately.) Cover the back of the first tile with adhesive, using a ¼" notched trowel.

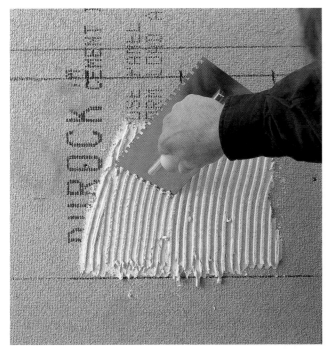

Variation: Spread adhesive on a small section of the wall, then set the tiles into the adhesive. Thin-set adhesive sets quickly, so work quickly if you choose this installation method.

3 Beginning near the center of the wall, apply the tile to the wall with a slight twisting motion, aligning it exactly with the horizontal and vertical reference lines. When placing cut tiles, position the cut edges where they will be least visible.

(continued next page)

4 Continue installing tiles, working from the center to the sides in a pyramid pattern. Keep the tiles aligned with the reference lines. If the tiles are not self-spacing, use plastic spacers inserted in the corner joints to maintain even grout lines (inset). The base row should be the last row of full tiles installed. Cut tile as necessary (see pages 40 to 41).

5 As small sections of tile are completed, "set" the tile by laying a scrap of 2 × 4 wrapped with carpet onto the tile and rapping it lightly with a mallet. This embeds the tile solidly in the adhesive and creates a flat, even surface.

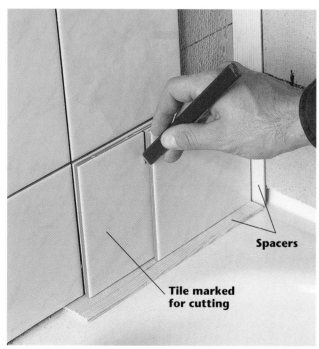

Spacers

Tile marked for cutting

6 To mark tiles for straight cuts, begin by taping ⅛" spacers against the surfaces below and to the side of the tile. Position a tile directly over the last full tile installed, then place a third tile so the edge butts against the spacers. Trace the edge of the top tile onto the middle tile to mark it for cutting.

7 Install any trim tiles, such as the bullnose edge tiles shown above, at border areas. Wipe away excess mortar along the top edges of the edge tiles. Use bullnose and corner bullnose (with two adjacent bullnose edges) tiles at outside corners to cover the rough edges of the adjoining tiles.

8 Let mortar dry completely (12 to 24 hours), then mix a batch of grout containing latex additive. Apply the grout with a rubber grout float, using a sweeping motion to force it deep into the joints. Do not grout joints adjoining bathtubs, floors, or room corners. These will serve as expansion joints and will be caulked later.

9 Wipe a damp grout sponge diagonally over the tile, rinsing the sponge in cool water between wipes. Wipe each area only once; repeated wiping can pull grout from the joints. Allow the grout to dry for about 4 hours, then use a soft cloth to buff the tile surface and remove any remaining grout film.

10 When the grout has cured completely, use a small foam brush to apply grout sealer to the joints, following the manufacturer's directions. Avoid brushing sealer on the tile surfaces, and wipe up excess sealer immediately.

11 Seal expansion joints at the floor and corners with silicone caulk. After the caulk dries, buff the tile with a dry, soft cloth.

Installing Wall Tile in a Bathtub Alcove

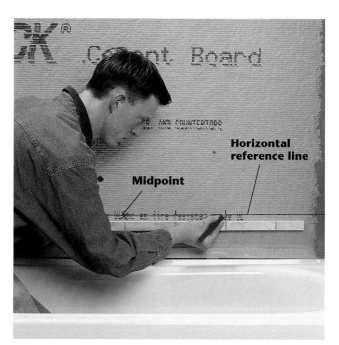

1 Beginning with the back wall, measure up and mark a point at a distance equal to the height of one ceramic tile (if the tub edge is not level, measure up from the lowest spot). Draw a level line through this point, along the entire back wall. This line represents a tile grout line and will be used as a reference line for making the entire tile layout.

2 Measure and mark the midpoint on the horizontal reference line. Using a story pole, mark along the reference line where the vertical grout joints will be located. If the story pole shows that the corner tiles will be less than half of a full tile width, move the midpoint half the width of a tile in either direction and mark (shown in next step).

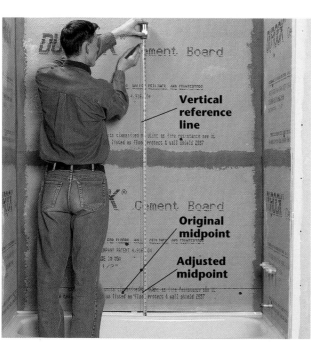

3 Use a level to draw a vertical reference line through the adjusted midpoint from the tub edge to the ceiling. Measure up from the tub edge along the vertical reference line and mark the rough height of the top row of tiles.

4 Use the story pole to mark the horizontal grout joints along the vertical reference line, beginning at the mark for the top row of tiles. If the cut tiles at the tub edge will be less than half the height of a full tile, move the top row up half the height of a tile. *Note:* If tiling to a ceiling, evenly divide the tiles to be cut at the ceiling and tub edge, as for the corner tiles.

5 Use a level to draw an adjusted horizontal reference line through the vertical reference line at a grout joint mark close to the center of the layout. This splits the tile area into four workable quadrants.

6 Use a level to transfer the adjusted horizontal reference line from the back wall to both side walls, then follow step 3 through step 6 to lay out both side walls. Adjust the layout as needed so the final column of tiles ends at the outside edge of the tub. Use only the adjusted horizontal and vertical reference lines for ceramic tile installation.

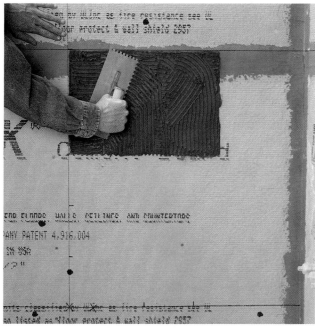

7 Mix a small batch of thin-set mortar containing a latex additive. (Some mortar has additive mixed in by the manufacturer and some must have additive mixed separately.) Spread adhesive on a small section of the wall, along both legs of one quadrant, using a ¼" notched trowel.

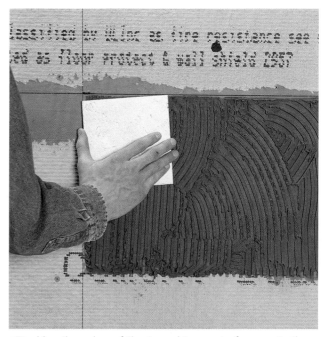

8 Use the edge of the trowel to create furrows in the mortar. Set the first tile in the corner of the quadrant where the lines intersect, using a slight twisting motion. Align the tile exactly with both reference lines. When placing cut tiles, position the cut edges where they will be least visible.

(continued next page)

9 Continue installing tiles, working from the center out into the field of the quadrant. Keep the tiles aligned with the reference lines and tile in one quadrant at a time. If the tiles are not self-spacing, use plastic spacers inserted in the corner joints to maintain even grout lines (inset). The base row against the tub edge should be the last row of tiles installed. To cut tiles at inside corners, see step 6 on page 156.

10 Install trim tiles, such as the bullnose tiles shown above, at border areas. Wipe away excess mortar along the top edges of the edge tiles.

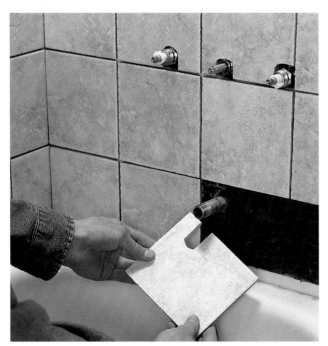

11 Mark and cut tiles to fit around all plumbing accessories or plumbing fixtures. Refer to pages 40 to 41 for tile cutting techniques.

12 Install any ceramic accessories by applying thin-set mortar to the back side, then pressing the accessory into place. Use masking tape to support the weight until the mortar dries (inset). Fill the tub with water, then seal expansion joints around the bathtub, floor, and corners with silicone caulk (see page 157).

Variation: Tiling Bathroom Walls

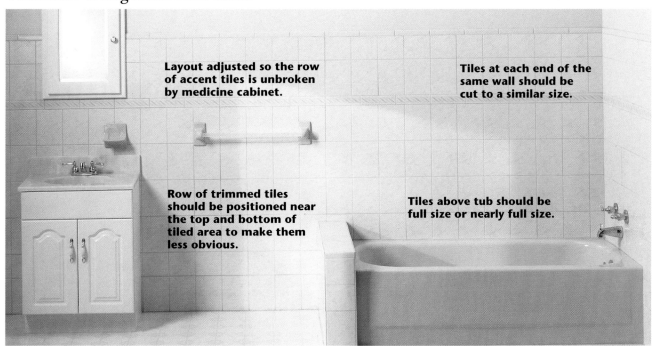

Layout adjusted so the row of accent tiles is unbroken by medicine cabinet.

Tiles at each end of the same wall should be cut to a similar size.

Row of trimmed tiles should be positioned near the top and bottom of tiled area to make them less obvious.

Tiles above tub should be full size or nearly full size.

Tiling an entire bathroom requires careful planning. The bathroom shown here was designed so that the tiles directly above the bathtub (the most visible surface) are nearly full height. To accomplish this, cut tiles were used in the second row up from the floor.

The short second row also allows the row of accent tiles to run uninterrupted below the medicine cabinet. Cut tiles in both corners should be of similar width to maintain a symmetrical look in the room.

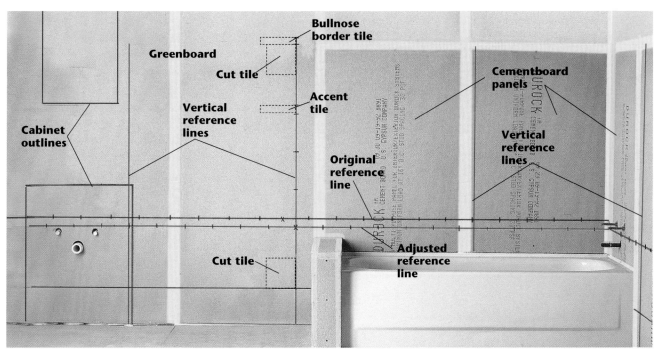

Bullnose border tile

Greenboard

Cut tile

Accent tile

Vertical reference lines

Cabinet outlines

Cementboard panels

Vertical reference lines

Original reference line

Adjusted reference line

Cut tile

The key to a successful wall-tile project is the layout. Mark the wall to show the planned location of all wall cabinets, fixtures, and wall accessories, then locate the most visible horizontal line in the bathroom, which is usually the top edge of the bathtub. Follow the steps on pages 87 to 91 to establish the layout, using a story pole to see how the tile pattern will run in relation to the other features in the room. After establishing the working reference lines, mark additional vertical reference lines on the walls every 5 to 6 tile spaces along the adjusted horizontal reference line to split large walls into smaller, workable quadrants, then install the tile. *Note:* Premixed, latex mastic adhesives generally are acceptable for wall tile in dry areas.

Tiling a Fireplace Surround

Tile dresses a fireplace surround in style—any style you like. From simple ceramic to elegant cut stone to handmade art tile, anything goes. As long as it's sturdy enough to withstand significant swings in temperature, almost any tile will work.

Although the project shown here starts with unfinished wallboard, you can tile over any level surface that's not glossy. If you're tiling over old tile or brick, go over the surface with a grinder, then apply a thin coat of latex-reinforced thin-set mortar to even out any irregularities. To rough up painted surfaces, sand them lightly before beginning the project.

The tile shown here is flush with the face of the firebox, which then supports it during installation. If necessary, tack battens in place to support the weight of your tile during installation. (Make sure the batten is level.)

You can finish the edges of the surround with wood cap rail trim, as shown here, bullnose tile, or other trim tile.

EVERYTHING YOU NEED

Tools: level, drill, hammer, nail set, V-notched trowel, grout float.

Materials: 2 × 4 lumber, mantel, tile, tile spacers, latex-reinforced thin-set mortar, masking tape, grout, cap rail trim, 6d and 4d finish nails, wood putty.

Mantel support cleat

1 To install the mantel, measure up from the floor and mark the height of the support cleat. Use a level to draw a level line through the mark. Mark the stud locations just above the level line. Position the cleat on the line, centered between the frame sides, and drill a pilot hole at each stud location. Fasten the cleat to the studs with screws provided by the manufacturer.

2 Paint the areas of wallboard that won't be tiled. Finish the mantel as desired, then fit it over the support cleat and center it. Drill pilot holes for 6d finish nails through the top of the mantel, about ¾" from the back edge. Secure the mantel to the cleat with four nails. Set the nails with a nail set, fill the holes with wood putty, then touch up the finish.

3 Dry-fit the tile around the front of the fireplace. You can lay tile over the black front face, but do not cover the glass or any portion of the grills. If you're using tile without spacer lugs, use spacers to set the gaps (at least ⅛" for floor tile). Mark the perimeter of the tile area and make any other layout marks that will help with the installation. Pre-cut tiles, if possible.

4 Mask off around the tile, then use a V-notched trowel to apply latex mastic tile adhesive to the wall, spreading it evenly just inside the perimeter lines. Set the tiles into the adhesive, aligning them with the layout marks, and press firmly to create a good bond. Install spacers as you work, and scrape out excess adhesive from the grout joints. Install all of the tile, then let the adhesive dry completely.

5 Mix a batch of grout and spread it over the tiles with a rubber grout float. Drag the float across the joints diagonally, tilting it at a 45° angle. Make another pass to remove excess grout. Wait 10 to 15 minutes, then wipe away excess grout with a damp sponge, rinsing frequently. Let the grout dry for one hour, then polish the tiles with a dry cloth. Let the grout dry completely.

6 Cut pieces of cap rail trim to fit around the tile, mitering the ends. If the tile is thicker than the trim recesses, install buildup strips behind the trim, using finish nails. Finish the trim to match the mantel. Drill pilot holes and nail the trim in place with 4d finish nails. Set the nails with a nail set. Fill the holes with wood putty and touch up the finish.

Tiling a Kitchen Backsplash

There are few spaces in your home with as much potential for creativity and visual impact as the 18" between your kitchen countertop and cupboards. A well-designed backsplash can transform an ordinary kitchen into something extraordinary.

Tiles for the backsplash can be attached directly to wallboard or plaster and do not require backerboard. When purchasing the tile, order 10 percent extra to cover breakage and cutting. Before installing, prepare the work area by removing switch and receptacle coverplates. Protect the countertop from scratches by covering it with a drop cloth.

EVERYTHING YOU NEED

Tools: level, tape measure, pencil, tile cutter, rod saw, notched trowel, rubber grout float, beating block, rubber mallet, sponge, bucket.

Materials: straight 1 × 2, wall tile, tile spacers (if needed), bullnose trim tile, mastic tile adhesive, masking tape, grout, caulk, drop cloth, grout sealer.

Tips for Planning Tile Layouts

Gather planning brochures and design catalogs to help you create decorative patterns and borders for the backsplash.

Break tiles into fragments and make a mosaic backsplash. Always use a sanded grout for joints wider than 1/8".

Add painted mural tiles to create a focal point. Mixing various tile styles adds an appealing contrast.

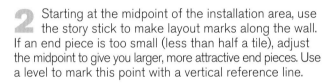

1 Make a story stick by marking a board at least half as long as the backsplash area to match the tile spacing.

2 Starting at the midpoint of the installation area, use the story stick to make layout marks along the wall. If an end piece is too small (less than half a tile), adjust the midpoint to give you larger, more attractive end pieces. Use a level to mark this point with a vertical reference line.

3 While it may appear straight, your countertop may not be level and therefore is not a reliable reference line. Run a level along the counter to find the lowest point on the countertop. Mark a point two tiles up from the low point and extend a level line across the entire work area.

(continued next page)

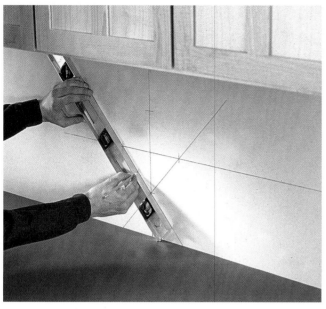

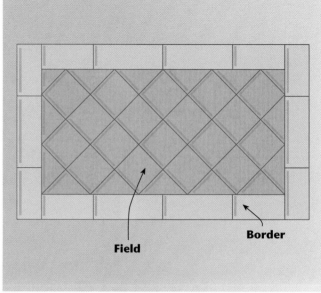

Field

Border

Variation: Diagonal Layout. Mark vertical and horizontal reference lines, making sure the angle is 90°. To establish diagonal layout lines, measure out equal distances from the crosspoint, then connect the points with a line. Additional layout lines can be extended from these as needed. To avoid the numerous, unattractive perimeter cuts common to diagonal layouts, try using a standard border pattern as shown. Diagonally set a field of full tiles only, then cut enough half tiles to fill out the perimeter. Finally, border the diagonal field with tiles set square to the field.

4 Apply mastic adhesive evenly to the area beneath the horizontal reference line, using a notched trowel. Comb the adhesive horizontally with the notched edge.

5 Starting at the vertical reference line, press tiles into the adhesive with a slight twisting motion. If the tiles are not self-spacing, use plastic spacers to maintain even grout lines. If the tiles do not hang in place, use masking tape to hold them in place until the adhesive sets.

6 Install a whole row along the reference line, checking occasionally to make sure the tiles are level. Continue installing tiles below the first row, trimming tiles that butt against the countertop as needed.

7 Apply adhesive to an area above the line and continue placing tiles, working from the center to the sides. Install trim tile, such as bullnose tile, to the edges of the rows.

8 When the tiles are in place, make sure they are flat and firmly embedded by laying a beating block against the tile and rapping it lightly with a mallet. Remove the spacers. Allow the mastic to dry for at least 24 hours, or as directed by the manufacturer.

9 Mix the grout and apply it with a rubber grout float. Spread it over the tiles, keeping the float at a low 30° angle, pressing the grout deep into the joints. *Note:* For grout joints ⅛" and smaller, be sure to use a non-sanded grout.

10 Wipe off excess grout, holding the float at a right angle to the tile, working diagonally so as not to remove grout from the joints. Clean any remaining grout from the tiles with a damp sponge, working in a circular motion. Rinse the sponge thoroughly and often.

11 Shape the grout joints by making slow, short, passes with the sponge, shaving down any high spots; rinse the sponge frequently. Fill any voids with a fingerful of grout. When the grout has dried to a haze, buff the tile clean with a soft cloth. Apply a bead of caulk between the countertop and tiles. Reinstall any electrical fixtures you removed. After the grout has completely cured, you may want to apply a grout sealer to help prevent discoloration.

Photo courtesy of Daltile

Counter Projects

(*above*) This countertop takes a slightly different tack on color banding. A dark border encompasses the edges of the counter and sink, the backsplash, and mirror. Although the border incorporates a number of different colors and textures, they have enough in common to stand together in contrast to the whites of the counter, sink, and vanity.

Simple touches like bands of color or texture focus attention on countertops.

(*above*) Solid blue V-cap anchors the edges of this blue and white countertop to the wall below. The same blue is repeated on the tub surround and the mirror frame.

(*opposite*) Geometric accent tiles draw all eyes to this backsplash and countertop made of natural looking porcelain tile.

(*above*) The raised design on the edges of this countertop complements the wall's elaborate shell motif without competing for attention.

Plain or fancy? Options abound for edge treatments, which deserve careful consideration during the planning phases of countertop projects.

(*above*) The decorative border at this counter's edge is repeated from the border at the base of the backsplash. This strategy tricks the eye into seeing the decorative edge as part of the border from some angles.

(*right*) V-cap protects the edges of this countertop and blends its color into the wood trim and the sleek cabinets below.

Each of these kitchen counters repeats a color or motif from elsewhere in the room.

(*opposite, top*) Here, white on white is the theme, presenting a clean, crisp background that can be accessorized in many ways over time. The textures in the wall tile and the profile of the countertop's V-cap keep this spare approach from becoming boring.

(*opposite, bottom*) The deep green borders in the backsplashes and countertops echo the kitchen chairs and other accessories in this spacious kitchen.

(*above*) The countertops on this kitchen island complement the wallpaper borders on the soffit and inside the recessed ceiling.

Building a Tile Countertop

Ceramic tile is a popular choice for countertops and backsplashes for a number of reasons. It's available in a vast range of sizes, styles, and colors; it's durable and can be repaired; and some tile—not all—is reasonably priced. With careful planning, tile is also easy to install; making a custom countertop is a good do-it-yourself project.

The best tile for most countertops is glazed ceramic floor tile. Glazed tile is better than unglazed because of its stain resistance, and floor tile is better than wall tile because it's harder and more durable. Most residential floor tile has a hardness rating of Class 3 or better. Porcelain tile also is suitable for countertops; it's very hard and durable, but typically much more expensive than ceramic tile.

While glazing protects tile from stains, the grout between tiles is still vulnerable because it's so porous. To minimize staining, use a grout that contains a latex additive, or mix the grout powder with a liquid latex additive instead of water. After the grout cures fully, apply a quality grout sealer, and reapply the sealer once a year thereafter.

The countertop in this project has a core of ¾" exterior-grade plywood that's cut to fit and fastened to the cabinets. (Treated plywood, particleboard, and oriented-strand board are not acceptable backers for this project.) The plywood is covered with a layer of plastic (for a moisture barrier) and a layer of ½"-thick cementboard. Cementboard is an effective backer for tile because it won't break down if water gets through the tile layer. The tile is adhered to the cementboard with thin-set adhesive, which also can survive prolonged water contact. The overall thickness of the finished countertop is about 1½". If you want a thicker countertop, you can fasten an additional layer of plywood (of any thickness) to the core.

When laying out the tile for your countertop, account for the placement of the sink and any other fixtures. The tile should break evenly where it meets the sink and along the counter's perimeter. If you'll be installing a tile-in sink, make sure the tile thickness matches the rim of the sink to create a smooth transition.

EVERYTHING YOU NEED

Tools: tape measure, circular saw, drill, utility knife, straightedge, stapler, drywall knife, framing square, notched trowel, tile cutter, carpeted 2 × 4, mallet, rubber grout float, sponge, foam brush, caulk gun.

Materials: ceramic tile, tile spacers, ¾" exterior-grade (CDX) plywood, 4-mil polyethylene sheeting, packing tape, ½" cementboard, 1¼" galvanized deck screws, fiberglass mesh tape, thin-set mortar, grout with latex additive, silicone caulk, silicone grout sealer.

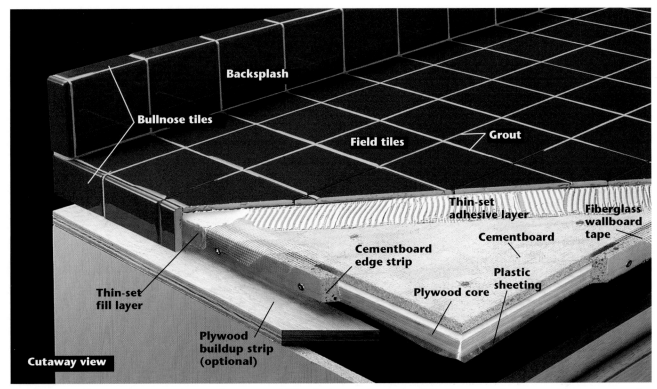

A ceramic tile countertop starts with a core of ¾" exterior-grade plywood that's covered with a moisture barrier of 4-mil polyethylene sheeting. Half-inch cementboard is screwed to the plywood, and the edges are capped with cementboard and finished with fiberglass mesh tape and thin-set mortar. Tiles for edging and backsplashes may be bullnose or another type of specialty tile (see below).

Options for Backsplashes & Countertop Edges

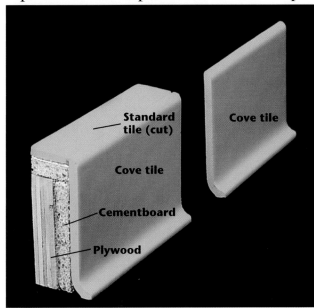

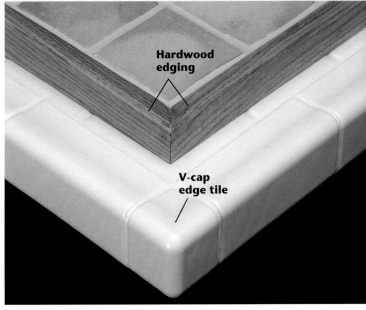

Backsplashes can be made from cove tile (right) attached to the wall at the back of the countertop. You can use the tile alone or build a shelf-type backsplash (left), using the same construction used for the countertop. Attach the plywood backsplash to the plywood core of the countertop. Wrap the front face and all edges of the plywood backsplash with cementboard before laying tile.

Edge options include V-cap edge tile and hardwood strip edging. V-cap tiles have raised and rounded corners that create a ridge around the countertop perimeter—good for containing spills and water. V-cap tiles must be cut with a tile saw. Hardwood strips should be prefinished with at least three coats of polyurethane finish. Attach the strips to the plywood core so the top of the wood will be flush with the faces of the tiles.

Building a Tile Countertop

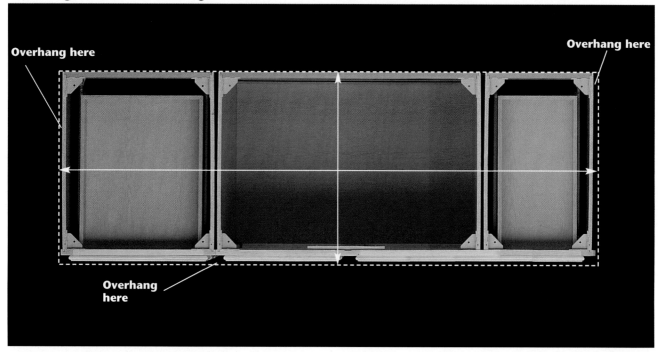

Overhang here

Overhang here

Overhang here

1 Determine the size of the plywood core by measuring across the top of the cabinets. The finished top should overhang the drawer fronts by at least ¼". Be sure to account for the thickness of the cementboard, adhesive, and tile when deciding how large to make the overhang. Cut the core to size from ¾" plywood, using a circular saw. Also make any cutouts for sinks and other fixtures (page 193).

Corner bracket

2 Set the plywood core on top of the cabinets, and attach it with screws driven through the cabinet corner brackets. The screws should not be long enough to go through the top of the plywood core.

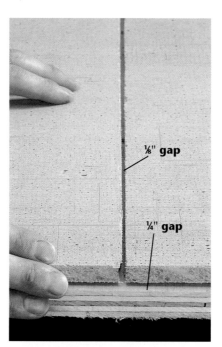

⅛" gap

¼" gap

3 Cut pieces of cementboard to size, then mark and make the cutout for the sink. Dry-fit them on the plywood core with the rough sides of the panels facing up. Leave a ⅛" gap between the cementboard sheets and a ¼" gap along the perimeter.

Tip: Cut cementboard using a straightedge and utility knife or a cementboard cutter with a carbide tip. Hold the straightedge along the cutting line, and score the board several times with the knife. Bend the piece backwards to break it along the scored line. Back-cut to finish.

4 Lay the plastic moisture barrier over the plywood core, draping it over the edges. Tack it in place with a few staples. Overlap seams in the plastic by 6", and seal them with packing tape.

5 Lay the cementboard pieces rough-side up on the plywood and attach them with cementboard screws driven every 6". Drill pilotholes using a masonry bit, and make sure all screw heads are flush with the surface. Wrap the countertop edges with 1¼"-wide cementboard strips, and attach them to the core with cementboard screws.

6 Tape all cementboard joints with fiberglass mesh tape. Apply three layers of tape along the front edge where the horizontal cementboard sheets meet the cementboard edging.

7 Fill all gaps and cover all of the tape with a layer of thin-set mortar. Feather out the mortar with a drywall knife to create a smooth, flat surface.

(continued next page)

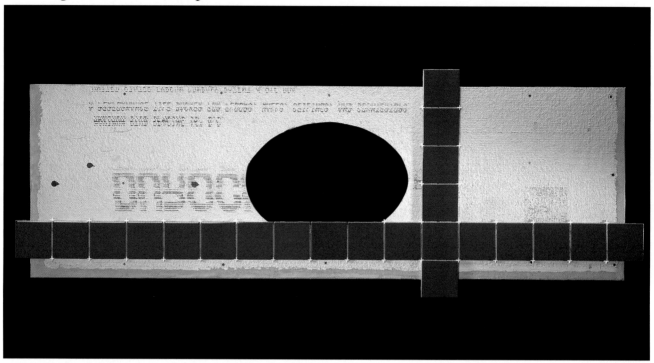

8 Dry-fit tiles on the countertop to find the layout that works best. If the tiles do not have spacing lugs on their edges, use plastic spacers to set the grout-joint gaps between tiles. Once the layout is established, make marks along the vertical and horizontal rows. Draw reference lines through the marks and use a framing square to make sure the lines are perpendicular.

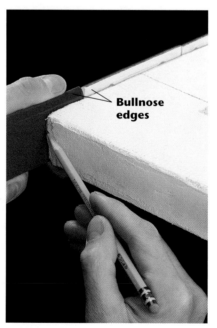

Bullnose edges

9 Install the edge tiles by applying a layer of thin-set mortar to the back of the tile and the edges of the countertop, using a notched trowel. Place the tiles with a slight twisting motion. Add plastic spacers, if needed. Use a dry tile set on top of the countertop to determine the height of the edge tiles.

10 Use bullnose corner tile (with adjacent bullnose edges) to finish the corner edges of the countertop. Place dry tile glazed-side down on the edge face. Mark and cut the tile so the bullnose edge will sit directly on the corner. Install the piece with thin-set mortar.

11 Install the field tile after the edge tiles have set. Spread a layer of thin-set on the cementboard along the layout lines, and install perpendicular rows of tile. Make sure the spacing is correct, and use a framing square to check your work as you go.

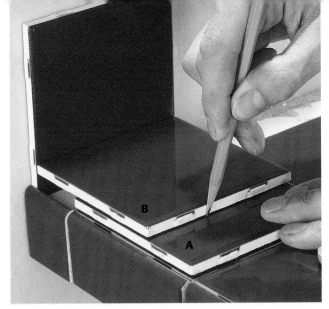

12 To mark border tiles for cutting, allow space for backsplash tiles, grout, and mortar by placing a tile against the back wall. Set another tile (A) on top of the last full tile in the field, then place a third tile (B) over tile A and hold it against the upright tile. Mark and cut tile A and install it with the cut edge toward the wall.

13 As you install small sections of tile, lay a carpeted 2 × 4 scrap over the tile and tap it lightly with a mallet. Run your hand over the tiles to make sure they are flush with one another. Remove any plastic spacers with a toothpick, and scrape any excess mortar from the grout joints. Let the mortar dry completely.

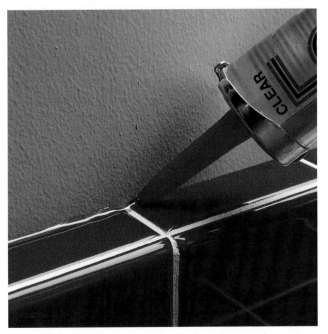

14 Mix a batch of grout with a latex additive and apply it with a rubber float, forcing the grout into the joints with a sweeping motion. Wipe away excess grout with a damp sponge. Wait one hour and wipe away the powdery haze. Let the grout cure fully.

15 Caulk along the backsplash and around penetrations with a fine bead of silicone caulk. Smooth the bead with a wet finger. After the grout cures completely, apply silicone sealer to the grout with a foam brush. Let the sealer dry, and apply a second coat.

Decorative Projects

Tile—alone or in combination with other materials—dresses ordinary objects in style and color.

(*above left*) The arm of this concrete garden bench holds a broken tile mosaic that combines the colors of water and sun.

(*above right*) Small mosaic art tiles lie among concentric circles of stone and shards. This idea could be translated to stepping stones, patios, or tabletops—let your imagination be your guide.

(*right*) Tile makes perfect coasters—no finish-damaging moisture can get past these charming little glass tile mosaics.

(*opposite*) This doorway trim is more ambitious than most decorative projects, but it's quite simple. Just set one row of tile around the doorway and finish the edges with wood trim. Outstanding!

184

(*above*) This plaster pedestal is decorated with whole and broken tiles. The scrollwork areas are painted with sanded grout that has been thinned with water.

Even mundane objects become artful when decorated with tile.

(*above*) For all practical purposes, typical stair risers are invisible. With their colorful handpainted tile, these risers are anything but typical and certainly not invisible.

(*opposite*) Art tile makes this bench one-of-a-kind. Adding tile to an existing bench is an extremely simple project, but even building the bench from scratch isn't difficult (see page 232).

(*above*) A broken tile mosaic transforms this small table into a unique accent piece. Tile can be applied to an existing tabletop or to a top cut from plywood.

Whole, broken, square, rectangular, or even round, tile adds color and interest to projects for your home and garden.

(*right*) A single hand-decorated tile adorns this iron table frame.

(*far right*) This terra-cotta saucer covered with mosaic tile showcases a few blossoms from the garden. It makes an equally interesting bird-bath or holder for floating candles.

(*above*) Mosaic tile can be pulled from its mesh backing and used to decorate pots and planters, with or without additional broken bits of tile.

(*opposite*) This lovely piece of artwork began as an inexpensive glass vase. It's easiest to glue tile fragments to pieces like this with hot glue or silicone caulk rather than traditional tile adhesives.

Creating Decorative Planters

The basic steps for adding tile to a planter are much the same as for adding tile to any other surface: Plan the layout, set and grout the tile. Fun and creativity come into the process when you turn your imagination loose with tile and containers.

Don't limit yourself to tile—mix in other materials such as flat glass marbles or broken pieces of stained glass,

EVERYTHING YOU NEED

Tools: snap cutter, tile nippers, putty knife, grout float, grout sponge.
Materials: 1" mosaic tile, tile mastic, grout, grout sealer.

mirror, and china. The designs can be as simple or as elaborate as you'd like.

Try a mosaic of daisies using bits of white stained glass for the petals, golden flat glass marbles for the centers, and broken tile bits for the background. Or maybe you'd prefer to use bits of green tile for a vine and leaves with purple flat glass marbles arranged like a bunch of grapes. Add a background of broken china or broken stained glass, and you've got a lot to show for a few hours' work.

Select containers that have flat rims like the white planter shown above or that have a broad expanse of flat surface like the pot shown in the project on page 191. Try to match the style and colors of the planters to the design.

1 Remove the mosaic tiles from their backing and experiment with designs and layouts. Cut tiles in half as necessary, using a snap cutter. Use tile nippers to break some tiles into small pieces.

2 Draw an irregular border around the planter, ranging from 1½" to 2" wide. Use a putty knife to spread mastic within the border and position the tile, alternating between the whole and half tiles all the way around the planter.

3 Fill in the remaining portion of the border with pieces of broken tile. Let the mastic dry according to manufacturer's directions. Grout the tile (see page 167 for information on grouting tile). If the planter will be used outdoors, apply grout sealer after the grout has fully cured.

Building a Tiled Sink Base

From its treadle sewing machine base to its handmade tile and hand-thrown sink, this project is unique. We used tile and a sink created by Kerry Brooks of Dock 6 Pottery, in Minneapolis, Minnesota (see Resources on page 246 for contact information). Other versions could be made with commercially available tile and one of the many bowl-type sinks on the market.

It isn't necessary to use a sewing machine stand, either. Many interesting or vintage pieces will work for the base. Don't destroy a valuable antique—instead, look for a stand with no top or a small chest with a badly damaged top. You'll need to remove the top anyway in order to add a plywood and cementboard core that can stand up to daily exposure to water.

After you choose a base, select a bowl-type sink basin and a specially-designed faucet, either wall- or counter-mounted. You'll need to tile the wall around a wall-mounted faucet; you'll need to make cutouts for a counter-mounted faucet. Even with a counter-mounted faucet such as the one shown here, you may want to add a small back-splash (see page 177).

If you don't like the idea of raw plywood being visible from beneath the sink, paint one side (the bottom) of the plywood before beginning to assemble the core. Coordinate the paint color with the tile and sink, so your project looks attractive from any angle.

EVERYTHING YOU NEED

Tools: circular saw, drill and hole saw, jig saw, utility knife, heavy-duty stapler, putty knife, framing square, trowel, grout float, grout sponge, foam brush, caulk gun, tape measure.

Materials: ¾" exterior-grade plywood, 4-mil plastic sheeting, packing tape, ½" cementboard, 1½" cementboard screws, fiberglass mesh, thin-set mortar, tile, grout and latex additive, caulk, salvaged base, bowl-type sink basin, faucet, drain hardware.

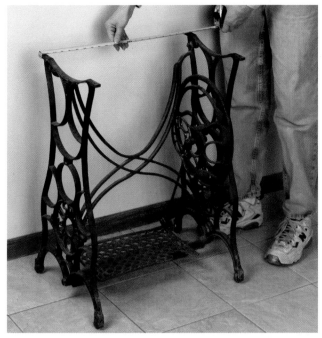

1 Measure the base and the sink and determine a size for the plywood core. Cut the core to size.

2 Mark a cutout for the sink on the plywood. Drill entrance holes, then use a jig saw to make the cutout. Use the template supplied with the faucet to mark those cutouts. Use a hole saw to make the faucet cutouts.

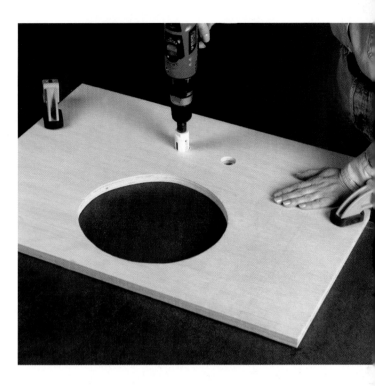

3 Cut cementboard to match the dimensions of the plywood core, then use the plywood as a template to mark the cutouts on the cementboard.

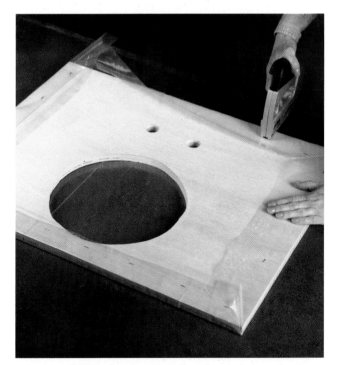

4 Lay plastic sheeting over the plywood core, draping it over the edges. Tack the plastic in place with staples. If you use more than one piece, overlap the seams by 6" and seal them with packing tape.

(continued next page)

5 Set the plywood core on top of the base and attach it with screws driven through the base and into the core. Use angle iron or L-brackets if necessary with the base you've selected. Make sure the screws don't go through the top of the plywood.

6 Position the cementboard (rough-side up) on the core and attach it with 1½" screws. Make sure the screwheads are flush with the surface. Cut 1¼"-wide cementboard strips and attach them to the edges of the core with screws.

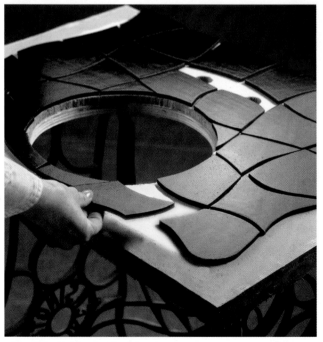

7 Tape all joints with fiberglass mesh. Apply three layers of tape along the edge where the top meets the edging. Fill all gaps and cover all of the tape with a layer of thin-set mortar. Feather out the mortar to create a smooth, flat surface.

8 Dry-fit tiles to find the layout, using spacers. Once the layout is established, make marks along the vertical and horizontal rows. Draw reference lines through the marks and use a framing square to make sure the lines are perpendicular.

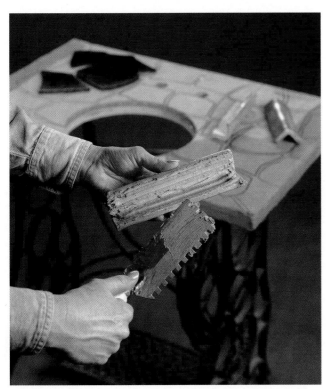

9 Set the edge tiles and let them dry. Install the field tiles and let them dry. Cut tile as necessary. See pages 176 to 181 for more information on setting tile.

10 Mix a batch of grout with a latex additive and apply it with a rubber grout float. Wipe away excess grout with a damp sponge (see page 181 for more information.) When the grout has cured, apply sealer with a foam brush.

11 Apply a bead of caulk to the side of the sink, just below the lip of the ridge. Set the sink into the cutout, resting the ridge of the sink at the lip of the cutout. Make sure the joint between the sink and the counter is filled with caulk.

12 Install the faucet and drain hardware, following manufacturer's instructions.

Building a Tiled Headboard

This headboard, designed to be reminiscent of a garden wall, is an effective combination of simple materials. Wallboard compound mixed with latex paint creates the appearance of stucco and 4 × 4 posts topped with deck post caps bring to mind an old-fashioned garden gate. Two rows of 2 × 2" tile complete the illusion. And even though this is a sophisticated project, it's very easy to build.

If you don't have lots of experience with wallboard compound, practice creating texture on scraps before you begin making the headboard. If you don't like the texture at first, you can keep working on it until you're satisfied. The texture should be fairly rough but without long spiky bits that might break off or—worse yet—poke an active sleeper.

The headboard in the photo above is adorned with a cast-resin cherub. We just embedded the hanging loop on the back of the cherub in hot glue, which held it quite securely. You could use silicone caulk if you prefer.

EVERYTHING YOU NEED

Tools: circular saw, jig saw, hammer, chisel, bar clamps, drill, snap cutter, tile nipper, drywall knife or 12" square trowel.

Materials: 4 × 4 cedar posts, ¾" plywood, 2 × 4s, 2½" drywall screws, latex paint, wallboard compound, masking tape, 2 × 2" ceramic tile, tile mastic, grout, deck post caps, grout sealer, bolts, semi-gloss polyurethane, Hollywood bed frame.

1 Clamp two cedar 4 × 4s together and mark cutting lines for the dadoes as shown in the diagram on page 198. Set the cutting depth on a circular saw to exactly match the thickness of the 2 × 4 stringers. Between the lines marked for the dadoes, make cuts across the posts, one cut every ¼". Use a chisel to remove the waste material within the dadoes. Set the stringers into position, their ends flush with the outside edges of the posts and their faces flush with the faces of the posts. Secure the stringers with 2½" drywall screws.

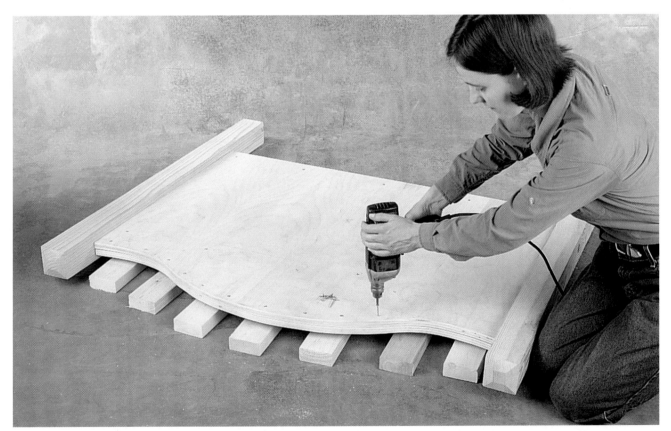

2 Cut the plywood base and backing. Mark the setting lines for the tile on the base. Screw the base to the stringers and countersink the screws. Turn the assembly over and set the backing in place above the first stringer; align its edges with the edges of the base. Secure the backing by driving screws into it through the front of the base. Countersink the screws. Mix paint into wallboard compound at a ratio of 1:4. Mask off the tile area, including the top edge of the assembly. Using a drywall knife or 12" square-end trowel, spread the paint/wallboard compound mixture onto the unmasked portion of the base and backing, and then onto the posts. Sweep across the compound, pressing down on one edge of the trowel or drywall knife to create a textured appearance. When the compound is completely dry, seal it with a coat of semi-gloss polyurethane.

(continued next page)

Building a Tiled Headboard, continued

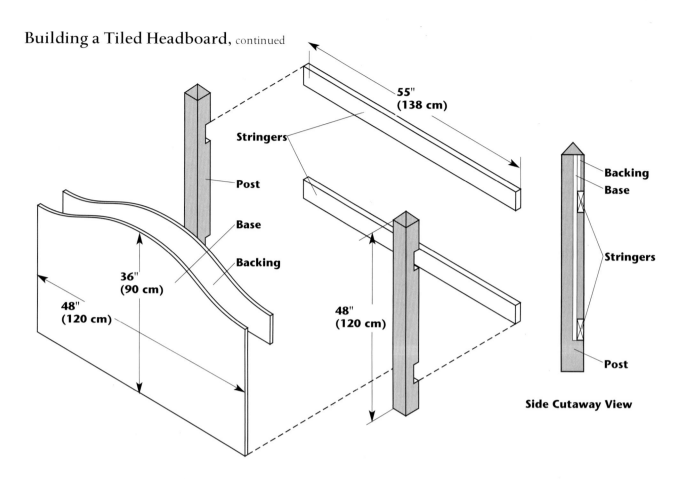

Stringers

Post

Base

Backing

55"
(138 cm)

36"
(90 cm)

48"
(120 cm)

48"
(120 cm)

Backing
Base

Stringers

Post

Side Cutaway View

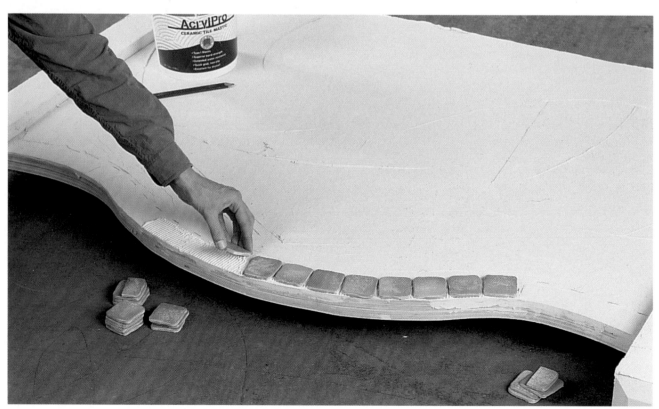

3 Lay out the tile and plan its placement. If necessary, use a snap cutter and nippers to trim the tile to fit.

4 Working on 18 to 24" at a time, spread mastic on the top of the unfinished plywood of the base and backing. Set the field tile flush with the edge of the base and then the edge tile flush with the face of the field tile. Press each tile firmly into the adhesive, twisting the tile slightly to settle it into place. Use hot glue to attach three tiles to each post, as shown on page 196.

5 When the tile adhesive is dry, mix grout and latex additive. Apply the grout, then wipe away the excess with a damp sponge. Rinse the sponge frequently and continue wiping until all the excess is removed. Let the grout dry for an hour, then polish the powdery film off of the tile. Allow the grout to cure as directed by the manufacturer before sealing it.

6 Mark and drill holes in the posts, then use bolts to attach a Hollywood bed frame to the headboard. Attach a deck post cap to each post.

Creating a Mosaic Wall Hanging

You no longer need to be an artist to create art from mosaic tiles. Mosaics have traditionally been created by artists who consider tile their medium, but now patterns for mosaics easily can be computer generated through specialized software.

The mosaic floor project on pages 130 to 135 takes you step-by-step through the process of generating a pattern. Here, we show you how to use that process to create a smaller mosaic to hang on a wall or display on a shelf. Wall mosaics typically are composed of ⅜" tile. We recommend glass tile, which is available in a range of colors and textures that lets you achieve subtle shading as well as amazing detail.

Despite the sophisticated results, this is a simple project. The one mildly tricky part is putting the mosaic mounting media onto the finished grids of tile. If the media wrinkles, the tile is displaced from the grid, which disturbs the spacing. To simplify the process, have someone help you. With one person holding each corner, press the media onto the tile, removing the backing gradually.

EVERYTHING YOU NEED

Tools: utility knife, straightedge, square trowel, grout float.

Materials: tile grids, ⅜" mosaic tiles, mosaic mounting media, tile mastic, grout, slot hangers.

1 Select an image and run it through the Tile Creator software (see pages 130 through 132). Identify the tiles according to the color chart and set up your workspace. Reading row by row, place a tile corresponding to each number on the printout in the grid. (Place the tiles right-side up.) Highlight each row of numbers as it's completed.

2 Remove the backing from the mosaic mounting media and smooth it onto the tiles (see page 134). Burnish the mounting media firmly to adhere it to the tiles.

3 Cut a piece of cementboard to the finished size of your mosaic. Measure the tile grids and mark off quadrants (see page 133). Spread mastic over one quadrant at a time and set the tile in place (with the mounting media on the top). Let the mastic dry, then peel the mounting media off the tile. Add tile to the edges.

4 Grout the tile (see pages 120 to 121). On the back of the mosaic, draw a straight line, 4" from the top. Install a slot hanger on each side, flush with the line and 4" in from the sides.

Creating an Address Marker Mosaic

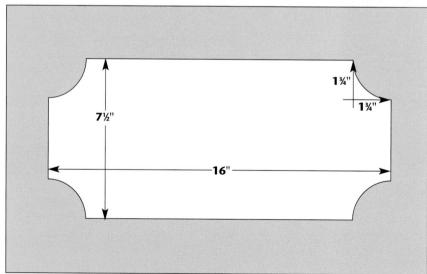

Broken tile and broken china combine beautifully for mosaics of all sorts. Here they're put to work on an address marker, a quick and easy project and a good way to use leftover tile.

Cut the marker in the shape shown here or create your own. No matter what shape you make it, be sure to use exterior-grade plywood and to seal the grout after it has cured according to manufacturer's directions. With those precautions, your address marker will remain attractive for many years.

EVERYTHING YOU NEED

Tools: jig saw, paintbrush, rubber mallet, tile nippers, rotary tool, hot glue gun, grout float, drill.

Materials: ¾" exterior-grade plywood, wood sealer, 4" number stencils, tile, chintz-patterned plates, hot glue or silicone caulk, grout, slot hangers and screws.

1 Enlarge and photocopy the pattern on the opposite
page. Trace the pattern onto plywood and cut it out,
using a jig saw. Apply a coat of wood sealer and let it
dry. Mark the center and draw parallel placement lines
on the plywood, then plan the placement of the numbers.
Trace the numbers onto the plywood, then draw a 1¼"
border around the outside edge.

2 Use a rotary tool and a grinding disc to polish away
the ridge on the back of each plate. One at a time,
place the plates in a heavy paper bag and roll the top
closed. Rap the bag with a rubber mallet to break the
plate. (Wear safety goggles.) Break the tiles in the same
manner.

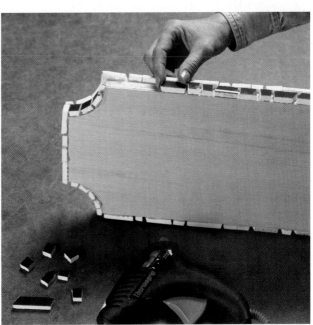

3 Lay out the pieces within the number outlines,
using tile nippers to reshape pieces as necessary.
Use hot glue or silicone caulk to secure the tile to the
plywood. Fill in the background with pieces of china.

4 Turn the marker on edge and add tile to all the
edges. Grout the tile, let it dry thoroughly, and seal
the grout with grout sealer. (See pages 120 to 121 for
more information on grouting tile.) Attach two slot
hangers to the back of the mosaic.

Outdoor Projects

Combined with other materials, tile works in surprising ways in outdoor settings.

(*right*) In this urban courtyard, stone tiles are spaced to allow moss to grow between them.

(*far right*) A long, spare table covered in bright blue tile makes an effective counterpoint to the neutral quarry tile floor and natural stone walls.

(*above*) In this alcove, decorative tiles grace a fireplace surround topped by a brick mantel. The floor combines large quarry tile with interesting accent tiles that emphasize the Mediterranean feeling of the patio. Accessories scattered throughout the area echo the blue-and-white theme set by the fireplace and accent tiles.

(*opposite*) A tiled fountain nestles into a flagstone patio, adding a welcome spot of color to the landscape in every season.

(*above*) The texture and mottled colors in this beautiful tile take a broad expanse of walkway far beyond its utilitarian purpose.

Seating areas, dining areas, walkways—even hot tubs—can be dressed up with tile.

(*above*) Variegated blue tile set on the diagonal transform a simple rectangular hot tub into something of an oasis in this backyard landscape.

(*opposite*) This raised patio floor is adorned with porcelain tile in a variety of sizes and shapes. The colors and textures of the tiles complement other elements of the scene, including the stone wall, the terra-cotta planters, and the weathered wood chair.

(*above*) This dining area is defined by the rug-like effect of a design area set into a border of larger tile set on the diagonal.

Coordinating colors between tile accents and a home's exterior multiplies their impact.

(*above*) The golden color of this home's exterior is reflected in the mottled colors of the tile patio and accented by the sunny yellow patio furniture.

(*right*) Navy blue and white diamonds extend the welcome of this inviting blue door.

(*opposite*) Blue, white, and yellow tiles surround a yellow and white trimmed window. Without this lovely treatment the window would be utterly unremarkable, but in combination with them, it's a star.

Plain or fancy, tile adds character and personality to outdoor floors.

(*above*) Each riser outfitted with its own design, this tiled staircase becomes an Italian-style showcase.

(*left*) The heraldic designs in these accent tiles bring to mind a courtyard in an English garden.

(*opposite*) Nothing more than two colors of plain rectangular tile, but this distinctive herringbone pattern produces the aura of sunshine and sea breezes.

Patio tile can turn a drab concrete slab into a charming outdoor living area. To create this tiled project, we first poured a new concrete subbase over an existing concrete patio (inset).

Finishing a Patio with Tile

The primary differences between interior and exterior tile are in the thickness of the tiles and the water-absorption rates. The project layout and application techniques are quite similar. For any type of tiling project, preparing or creating a suitable subbase for the tiles can become a fairly intensive project. A sturdy subbase is critical.

Patio tile is most frequently applied over a concrete subbase—either an existing concrete patio, or a new concrete slab. A third option, which we show you on the following pages, is to pour a new tile subbase over an existing concrete patio. This option involves far less work and expense than removing an old patio and pouring a new slab. And it ensures that your new tiled patio will not develop the same problems that may be present in the existing concrete surface. See the photographs at the top of

page 216 to help you determine the best method for preparing an existing concrete patio for tile.

If you do not have a concrete slab in the project area already, you will need to pour one or have one poured.

The patio tiling project shown here is divided into two separate projects: pouring a new subbase and installing patio tile. If you have an existing patio in good condition, you do not need to pour a new subbase.

When selecting tiles for your patio, make sure the product you purchase is exterior tile, which is designed to withstand freezing and thawing better than interior tile. Try to select colors and textures that match or complement other parts of your house and yard. If your project requires extensive tile cutting, rent a wet saw or arrange to have the tiles cut to size at the supply center.

Exterior tile products for patios are denser and thicker than interior tile. Common types include shell-stone tile, ceramic patio tile, and quarry tile. The most common size is 12" × 12", but you also can purchase precut designer tiles that are assembled into elaborate patterns and designs.

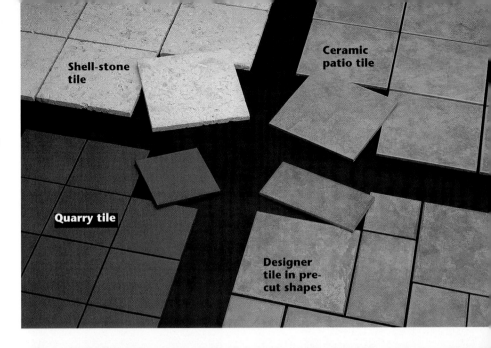

Tools for working with exterior tile include: a wet saw for cutting large amounts of tile (usually a rental item), a square-notched trowel for spreading tile adhesive (consult the tile manufacturer's instructions regarding the proper notch size), a grout float for spreading grout into joints between tiles, a sponge for wiping up excess grout, tile nippers for making curved or angled cuts in tiles, tile spacers to set standard joints between tiles, and a rubber mallet for setting tiles into adhesive.

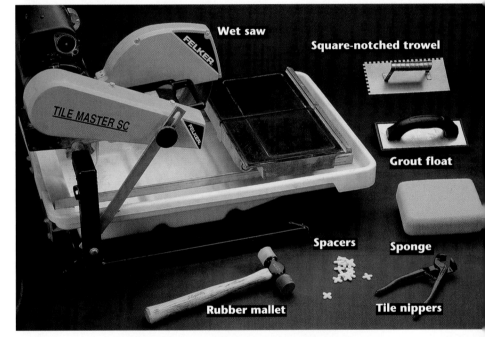

Materials for installing patio tile include: exterior tile grout (tinted or untinted), acrylic grout sealer, metal stucco lath as reinforcement for concrete slab, latex caulk for filling tile joints over control joints, caulk backer rod to keep grout out of control joints during grout application, latex-fortified grout additive, tile sealer, floor-mix concrete for building a tile subbase, tile adhesive (dry-set mortar), and a mortar bag for filling joints with grout (optional).

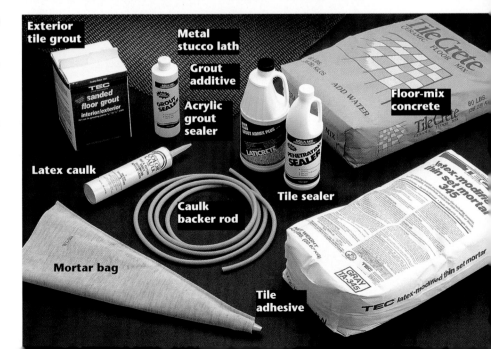

Tips for Evaluating Concrete Surfaces

A good surface is free from any major cracks or badly flaking concrete (called spalling). You can apply patio tile directly over a concrete surface that is in good condition if it has control joints (see below).

A fair surface may exhibit minor cracking and spalling, but has no major cracks or badly deteriorated spots. Install a new concrete subbase over a surface in fair condition before laying patio tile.

A poor surface contains deep or large cracks, broken, sunken, or heaved concrete, or extensive spalling. If you have this kind of surface, remove the concrete completely and replace it with a new concrete slab before you lay patio tile.

Tips for Cutting Control Joints in a Concrete Patio

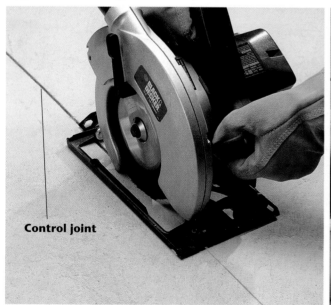

Control joint

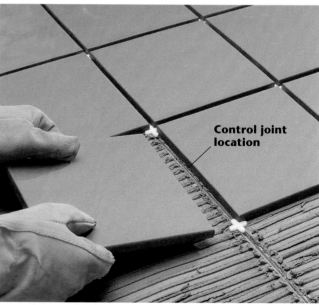

Control joint location

Cut new control joints into existing concrete patios that are in good condition but do not have enough control joints. Control joints allow inevitable cracking to occur in locations that don't weaken the concrete or detract from its appearance. They should be cut every 5 or 6 ft. in a patio. Plan the control joints so they will be below tile joints once the tile layout is established. Use a circular saw with a masonry blade set to ⅜" depth to cut control joints. Cover the saw base with duct tape to prevent it from being scratched.

Installing a Subbase for Patio Tile

EVERYTHING YOU NEED

Tools: basic hand tools, shovel, maul, straight-edge, aviation snips, masonry hoe, mortar box, hand tamper, magnesium float, concrete edger, utility knife, putty knife.

Materials: 30# building paper, plastic sheeting, 2 × 4 and 2 × 2 lumber, 2½" and 3" deck screws, ⅜" stucco lath, floor-mix concrete, roofing cement.

1 Dig a trench at least 6" wide, and no more than 4" deep, around the patio to create room for 2 × 4 forms. Clean dirt and debris from the exposed sides of the patio. Cut and fit 2 × 4 frames around the patio, joining the ends with 3" deck screws. Cut wood stakes from 2 × 4s and drive them next to the forms, at 2-ft. intervals.

2 Adjust the form height: set stucco lath on the surface, then set a 2 × 2 spacer on top of the lath (their combined thickness equals the thickness of the subbase). Adjust the form boards so the tops are level with the 2 × 2, and screw the stakes to the forms with 2½" deck screws.

3 Remove the 2 × 2 spacers and stucco lath, then lay strips of 30# building paper over the patio surface, overlapping seams by 6", to create a bond-breaker for the new surface. Crease the building paper at the edges and corners, making sure the paper extends past the tops of the forms. Make a small cut in the paper at each corner for easier folding.

4 Lay strips of stucco lath over the building paper bond-breaker, overlapping seams by 1". Keep the lath 1" away from the forms and the wall. Use aviation snips to cut the stucco lath (wear heavy gloves when handling metal).

(continued next page)

Screed board

5 Build temporary 2 × 2 forms to divide the project into working sections and provide rests for the screed board used to level and smooth the fresh concrete. Make the sections narrow enough that you can reach across the entire section (3-ft. to 4-ft. sections are comfortable for most people). Screw the ends of the 2 × 2s to the form boards so the tops are level.

6 Mix dry floor-mix concrete with water in a mortar box, blending with a masonry hoe, according to the manufacturer's directions, or use a power mixer.

Note: The mixture should be very dry when prepared so it can be pressed down into the voids in the stucco lath with a tamper.

7 Fill one working section with floor-mix concrete, up to the tops of the forms. Tamp the concrete thoroughly with a lightweight tamper to help force it into the voids in the lath and into corners. The lightweight tamper shown above is made from a 12" × 12" piece of ¾" plywood, with a 2 × 4 handle attached.

8 Level off the surface of the concrete by dragging a straight 2 × 4 screed board across the top, with the ends riding on the forms. Move the 2 × 4 in a sawing motion as you progress, creating a level surface and filling any voids in the concrete. If voids or hollows remain, add more concrete and smooth it off.

9 Use a magnesium float to smooth the surface of the concrete. Applying very light pressure, move the float back and forth in an arching motion, tipping the lead edge up slightly to avoid gouging the surface.

10 Pour and smooth out the next working section, repeating steps 7 to 9. After floating this section, remove the 2 × 2 temporary form between the two sections. Fill the void left behind with fresh concrete. Float the fresh concrete with the magnesium float until the concrete is smooth and level and blends into the working section on each side. Pour and finish the remaining working sections one at a time, using the same techniques.

(continued next page)

11 Let the concrete dry until pressing the surface with your finger does not leave a mark. Cut contours around all edges with a concrete edger. Tip the lead edge of the edger up slightly to avoid gouging the surface. Smooth out any marks left by the edger using a float.

12 Cover the concrete with sheets of plastic, and cure for at least three days (see manufacturer's directions for recommended curing time). Weight down the edges of the sheeting. After curing is compete, remove the plastic and disassemble and remove the forms.

13 Trim off the building paper using a utility knife. Apply roofing cement to three sides of the patio, using a trowel or putty knife to fill and seal the seam between the old and new surfaces. To provide drainage for moisture between layers, do not seal the lowest side of the patio. After the roofing cement dries, shovel dirt back into the trench around the patio.

Laying Patio Tile

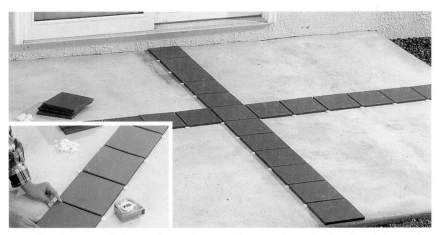

1 Dry-fit rows of tile on the surface so they run in each direction, intersecting at the center of the patio. Slip tile spacers between tiles to represent joints (inset). Keep the tiles ¼" to ½" away from the house to allow for expansion. This dry fit helps you establish and mark an attractive, efficient layout for the tile.

As with an indoor tiling project, creating and marking the layout lines and pattern for the tile is an important part of an exterior project. The best way to do this is to perform a dry run using the tiles you will install. Try to find a layout that requires the least possible amount of cutting.

Some patio tile is fashioned with small ridges on the edges that automatically establish the spacing between tiles. But more often, you will need to insert plastic spacers. The spacers should be removed before the tile adhesive dries.

Tiled patios are vulnerable to cracking. Make sure the tile subbase has sufficient control joints to keep cracking in check (page 216). Install tiles so the tile joints align with the control joints. Fill the tile joints over the control joints with flexible latex caulk, rather than grout.

2 Adjust the tile to create a layout that minimizes tile cutting. Shift the rows of tiles and spacers until the overhang is equal at each end and any cut portions are less than 2" wide.

EVERYTHING YOU NEED

Tools: carpenter's square, straight-edge, tape measure, chalk line, tile cutter or wet saw, tile nippers, square-notched trowel, needle-nose pliers, rubber mallet, grout float, grout sponge, caulk gun.

Materials: tile spacers, buckets, paintbrush and roller, plastic sheeting, paper towels, dry-set mortar, tile, backer rod, grout, grout additive, latex tile caulk, grout sealer, tile sealer.

Snap chalk line for reference

3 Once the layout is set, mark layout lines onto the surface. Mark at the joint between the third and fourth row out from the house, then measure the distance and mark it at several more points along the project area. Snap a chalk line to connect the marks.

(continued next page)

Laying Patio Tile, continued

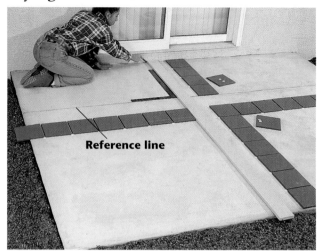

Reference line

4 Use a carpenter's square and a long, straight board to mark end points for a second reference line perpendicular to the first. Mark the points next to the dry-fit tile so the line falls on a joint location. Remove tools and tiles, and snap a chalk line that connects the points.

5 Lay tiles in one quadrant at a time, beginning with a section next to the house. Start by mixing a batch of dry-set mortar in a bucket, according to the manufacturer's directions. Spread mortar evenly along both legs of one quadrant using a square-notched trowel. Apply enough mortar for four tiles along each leg.

6 Use the edge of the trowel to create furrows in the mortar. Make sure you have applied enough mortar to completely cover the area under the tiles without covering up the reference lines.

7 Set the first tile in the corner of the quadrant where the lines intersect, pressing down lightly and twisting slightly from side to side. Adjust the tile until it is exactly aligned with both reference lines.

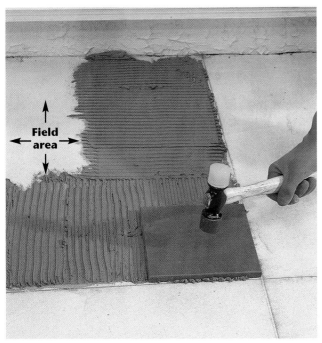

8 Rap the tile gently with a rubber mallet to set it. Rap evenly across the entire surface area, being careful not to break the tile or completely displace the mortar beneath the tile. *Note:* Once you start to fill in the field of the quadrant, it is faster to place several tiles at once, then set them all with the mallet at one time.

9 Set plastic spacers at the corners of the tile that face the working quadrant.

10 Position the next tile into the mortar bed along one arm of the quadrant, making sure the tiles fit neatly against the spacers. Rap the tile with the mallet to set it into the mortar, then position and set the next tile on the other leg of the quadrant. Make certain the tiles align with the reference lines.

11 Install the rest of the tile in the mortared area of the quadrant using the spacers to maintain uniform joints between tiles. Wipe off any excess mortar before it dries. *Note:* Plastic spacers are temporary: remove them before the mortar hardens—usually within one hour.

(continued next page)

Laying Patio Tile, continued

12 Apply a furrowed layer of mortar to the field area: do not cover more area than you can tile in 15 to 20 minutes. *Tip:* Start with smaller sections, then increase the size as you get a better idea of your working pace.

13 Set tiles into the field area of the first quadrant, saving any cut tiles for last. Rent a wet saw from your local rental store for cutting tiles, or use a tile cutter. For curved cuts, use tile nippers.

14 Apply mortar and fill in tiles in the next quadrant against the house, using the same techniques used for the first quadrant. Carefully remove plastic spacers with needlenose pliers as you finish each quadrant—do not leave spacers in mortar for more than one hour. Make sure to clean all excess mortar from the tiles before it hardens.

15 Fill in the remaining quadrants. *Tip:* Use a straight-edge to check the tile joints occasionally. If you find that any of the joint lines are out of alignment, compensate for the misalignment over several rows of tiles.

16 After all the tiles for the patio are set, check to make sure all spacers are removed and any excess mortar has been cleaned from the tile surfaces. Cover the project area with plastic for three days to allow the mortar to cure properly.

Caulking backer rod

17 After three days, remove the plastic and prepare the tile for grouting. Create expansion joints on the tiled surface by inserting strips of ¼"-diameter caulking backer rod into the joints between quadrants and over any control joints, to keep grout out of these joints.

(continued next page)

18 Mix a batch of tile grout and add latex grout additive. Starting in a corner and working out, pour a layer of grout onto an area of the surface that is 25 sq. ft. or less in size. Use a rubber grout float to spread the grout and pack it into the joints between tiles.

19 Use the grout float to scrape off excess grout. Scrape diagonally across the joints, holding the float in a near-vertical position. Patio tile will absorb grout quickly and permanently, so it is important to remove all excess grout from the surface before it sets. It's a good idea to have help when working on large areas.

20 Use a damp sponge to wipe the grout film from the surface of the tile. Rinse the sponge out frequently with cool water, and be careful not to press down so hard around joints that you disturb the grout. Wash grout off of the entire surface.

21 Let the grout dry for about four hours, then poke it with a nail to make sure it has hardened. Use a cloth to buff the tile surface until any remaining grout film is gone. If buffing does not remove all the film, try using a coarser cloth, such as burlap, or even an abrasive pad.

22 Remove the caulking backer rod from the expansion joints, then fill the joints with caulk that is tinted to match the grout color closely. The caulk will allow for some expansion and contraction of the tiled surface, preventing cracking and buckling.

23 Apply grout sealer to the grout lines using a sash brush or small sponge brush. Avoid spilling over onto the tile surface with the grout sealer. Wipe up any spills immediately.

24 After one to three weeks, seal the surface with tile sealer, following the manufacturer's applica- tion directions. A paint roller with an extension pole is a good tool for applying tile sealer.

227

Creating a Ceramic Tile Fountain

A fountain is welcome in any landscape, and building and installing one is easier and much less expensive than you might imagine. Think of it: a colorful tile-covered fountain reflected in a small garden pond, water gently splashing on sparkling sea glass. And you can make one. Easily.

Start with a common chimney flue tile and a few square feet of colorful mosaic tiles. Add an inexpensive twelve-volt fountain pump and tiny submersible disc lights, which can be wired into any low-voltage system. Almost before you know it, you'll be ready to show off for the neighbors.

One note of caution: before adding accessories to your low-voltage system, make sure your transformer can handle the extra load.

Chimney flue tiles are available in many different sizes and can be purchased at most fireplace and masonry stores. Small precut sheets of expanded metal grate are available from most hardware stores and home centers.

EVERYTHING YOU NEED

Tools: notched trowel, grout float, caulk gun, jig saw or bolt cutters.

Materials: 18 × 18 × 24" chimney flue tile, bricks, metal L-brackets, 18 × 18" expanded metal grate, 12 sq. ft. of mosaic tile, thinset-mortar, grout, concrete block, construction adhesive, low-voltage fountain pump, low-voltage fountain lights, sea glass (approx. 4 lbs.), silicone caulk.

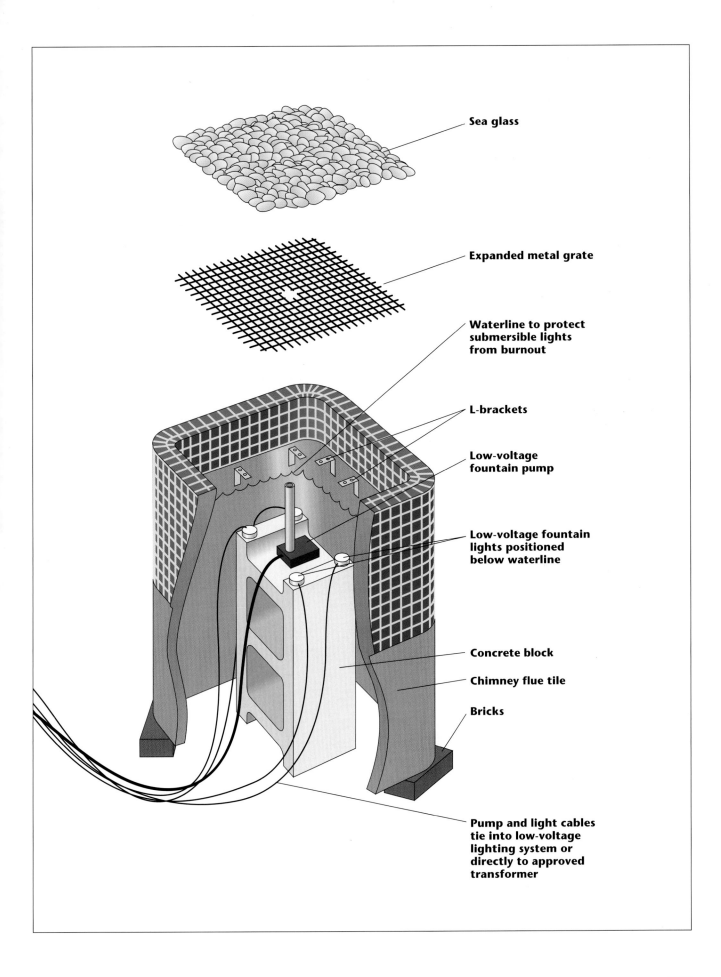

Sea glass

Expanded metal grate

Waterline to protect submersible lights from burnout

L-brackets

Low-voltage fountain pump

Low-voltage fountain lights positioned below waterline

Concrete block

Chimney flue tile

Bricks

Pump and light cables tie into low-voltage lighting system or directly to approved transformer

Creating a Ceramic Tile Fountain

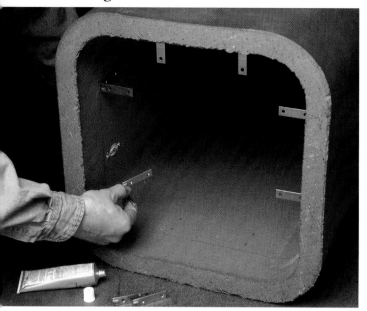

1 Draw a line on the inside of the flue tile, about 4" from the top. On each wall of the tile, position two L-brackets at the line and glue each bracket in place with construction adhesive.

2 Set tile on the outside of the flue tile and the inside down to the line. Working on one side of the flue at a time, spread thin-set mortar on the surface, then press the tile into place. Let the mortar dry according to manufacturer's directions. When the mortar is dry, grout the tile. (See pages 120 and 121 for information on grouting tile.)

3 Position four bricks at the bottom of the water garden and set the flue tile on them. (The flue tile will be very heavy—recruit a helper or two for this.) Set a concrete block in the center of the flue tile and put the fountain pump on top of it.

4 Set the lights in place, securing them to the concrete block with dabs of silicone caulk. Run the cables from the pump and lights out of the pond to the nearest fixture in your low-voltage lighting system. (If you don't have a low-voltage lighting system, run the cables to the transformer and plug the transformer into the nearest GFCI outlet.)

5 Connect the cables from the pump and lights to a cable from your low-voltage lighting system, using the simple connectors included with the pump. Add water to the pond and test the lights and pump. Adjust the operation of the pump as necessary. Dig a small, shallow trench and bury the cables.

6 If necessary, cut the expanded metal grate to fit inside the flue tile, using a jig saw with a metal-cutting blade. In the center of the grate, use the jig saw or a bolt cutter to expand a hole to approximately 2" in diameter. Insert the pump's discharge tube into this hole, then set the grate on top of the L-brackets in the flue tile. Mound the sea glass around the discharge tube. Use silicone to stick individual pieces of sea glass together, if necessary to hold them in place. Cover the remaining grate with a layer of sea glass.

Low-voltage Accessories

If you have a low-voltage lighting system, add light fixtures to the area surrounding your garden pond and fountain. The extra light will focus even more attention on this lovely little fountain.

Before adding additional fixtures and accessories, make sure your transformer can handle the extra load. If not, run the pond lighting as a separate circuit or purchase a larger transformer to handle the load.

Building a Tiled Garden Bench

Here's a splendid example of the term "return on investment." Four decorative tiles and a handful of coordinated accent tiles produce quite an impact. In fact, those accents and a few dozen 4 × 4" tiles transform a plain cedar bench into a special garden ornament. And you can accomplish the whole thing over one weekend.

EVERYTHING YOU NEED

Tools: tape measure, circular saw, drill, stapler, power or hand miter saw (optional), utility knife, chalk line, ¼" notched trowel, needlenose pliers, grout float, sponge.

Materials: 2 cedar 2 × 4s (8 ft.), 1 cedar 2 × 6 (8 ft.), 1 cedar 4 × 4 (8 ft.), 4 × 4 ft. sheet of ¾" exterior plywood, 4 × 4 ft. sheet of ½" cementboard, plastic sheeting, 2" galvanized deck screws, 3" galvanized deck screws, 1¼" cementboard screws, clear sealer, field and accent tile, thin-set mortar, tile spacers, grout, grout sealer.

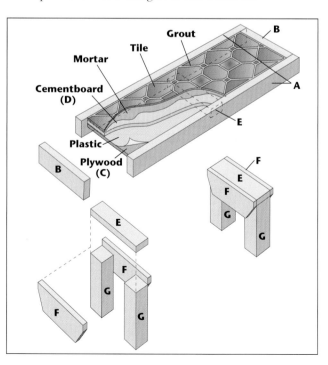

CUTTING LIST

Key	Part	Dimension	Pcs.	Material
A	Sides	1½ × 3½ × 51"	2	Cedar
B	Ends	1½ × 3½ × 16"	2	Cedar
C	Core	15 × 48"	1	Ext. Plywood
D	Core	15 × 48"	1	Cementboard
E	Stretchers	1½ × 3½ × 16"	3	Cedar
F	Braces	1½ × 5½ × 16"	4	Cedar
G	Legs	3½ × 3½ × 13"	4	Cedar

1 Cut two sides and two ends, then position the ends between the sides so the edges are flush. Make sure the frame is square. Drill ⅛" pilot holes through the sides and into the ends. Drive 3" screws through the pilot holes.

2 Cut three stretchers. Mark the sides, 4½" from the inside of each end. Using 1½" blocks beneath them as spacers, position the stretchers and make sure they're level. Drill pilot holes and fasten the stretchers to the sides with 3" screws.

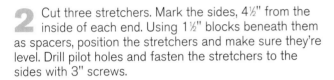

3 Cut one 15 × 48" core from ¾" exterior-grade plywood and another the same size from cementboard. Staple plastic sheeting over the plywood, draping it over the edges. Lay the cementboard rough-side up on the plywood and attach it with 1¼" cementboard screws driven every 6". Make sure the screw heads are flush with the surface.

4 Position the bench frame upside down and over the plywood/cementboard core. Drill pilot holes and then drive 2" galvanized deck screws through the stretchers and into the plywood.

(continued next page)

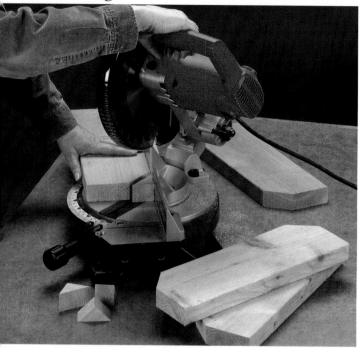

5 Cut four braces from a cedar 2 × 6. Mark the angle on each end of each brace by measuring down 1½" from the top edge and 1½" along the bottom edge. Draw a line between the two points and cut along that line, using a power or hand miter saw or a circular saw.

6 On each brace, measure down ¾" from the top edge and draw a reference line across the stretcher for the screw positions. Drill ⅛" pilot holes along the reference line. Position a brace on each side of the end stretchers and fasten them with 3" screws driven through the braces and into the stretchers.

7 Cut four 13" legs from a 4 × 4. Position each leg between a set of braces and against the sides of the bench frame. Drill pilot holes through each brace and attach the leg to the braces by driving 3" screws through the braces and into the leg. Repeat the process for each leg. Sand all surfaces with 150-grit sandpaper, then seal all wood surfaces with clear wood sealer.

8 Snap perpendicular reference lines to mark the center of the length and width of the bench. Beginning at the center of the bench, dry-fit the field tiles; include spacers. Set the accent tile in place and mark the field tile for cutting.

9 Cut the field tile and continue dry-fitting the bench top, including the accent and border tiles. When you're satisfied, remove the tile and apply thin-set mortar over the cementboard, using a notched trowel.

10 Set the tile into the thin-set mortar, using a slight twisting motion. Continue adding thin-set and setting the tile until the bench top is covered. Remove the spacers. Let the mortar dry according to manufacturer's directions. (See pages 118 to 119 for more information on setting tile.)

11 Mix grout and use a grout float to force it into the joints surrounding the tile. Wipe excess grout away with a damp sponge. When the grout has dried slightly, polish the tiles with a clean, dry cloth to remove the slight haze of grout. (See pages 120 to 121 for more information on grouting tile.)

Repair Projects

Maintaining Wall Tile

As we've said throughout this book, ceramic tile is durable and nearly maintenance-free, but like every other material in your house, it can fail or develop problems. The most common problem with ceramic tile involves damaged grout. Failed grout is unattractive, but the real danger is that it offers a point of entry for water. Given a chance to work its way beneath grout, water can destroy a tile base and eventually wreck an entire installation. It's important to regrout ceramic tile as soon as you see signs of damage.

Another potential problem for tile installations is damaged caulk. In tub and shower stalls and around sinks and backsplashes, the joints between the tile and the fixtures are sealed with caulk. The caulk eventually deteriorates, leaving an entry point for water. Unless the joints are recaulked, seeping water will destroy the tile base and the wall.

In bathrooms, towel rods, soap dishes, and other accessories can work loose from walls, especially if they weren't installed correctly or aren't supported properly. For maximum holding power, anchor new accessories to wall studs or blocking. If no studs or blocking are available, use special fasteners, such as toggle bolts or molly bolts, to anchor the accessories directly to the surface of the underlying wall. To hold screws firmly in place in ceramic tile walls, drill pilot holes and insert plastic sleeves, which expand when screws are driven into them.

EVERYTHING YOU NEED

Tools: awl, utility knife, trowel, grout float, hammer, chisel, small pry bar, eye protection.

Materials: replacement tile, tile adhesive, masking tape, grout, cloth or rag, rubbing alcohol, mildew remover, silicone or latex caulk, sealer.

Regrouting Wall Tile

1 Use an awl or utility knife to scrape out the old grout completely, leaving a clean bed for the new grout.

2 Clean and rinse the grout joints, then spread grout over the entire tile surface, using a rubber grout float or sponge. Work the grout well into the joints and let it set slightly.

3 Wipe away excess grout with a damp sponge. When the grout is dry, wipe away the residue and polish the tiles with a dry cloth.

Recaulking a Joint

1 Start with a completely dry surface. Scrape out the old caulk and clean the joint with a cloth dipped in rubbing alcohol. If this is a bathtub or sink, fill it with water to weight it down.

2 Clean the joint with a product that kills mildew spores; let it dry. Fill the joint with silicone or latex caulk.

3 Wet your fingertip with cold water, then use your finger to smooth the caulk into a cove shape. After the caulk hardens, use a utility knife to trim away any excess.

Replacing Built-in Wall Accessories

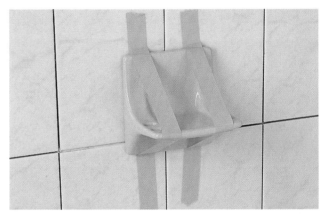

1 Carefully remove the damaged accessory (see page 240). Scrape away any remaining adhesive or grout. Apply dry-set tile adhesive to the back side of the new accessory, then press it firmly in place.

2 Use masking tape to hold the accessory in place while the adhesive dries. Let the mortar dry completely (12 to 24 hours), then grout and seal the area.

Replacing Surface-mounted Accessories

1 Lift the accessory up and off the mounting plate. If the mounting plate screws are driven into studs or blocking, simply hang the new accessory. If not, add hardware such as molly bolts, toggle bolts, or plastic anchor sleeves.

2 Put a dab of silicone caulk over the pilot holes and the tips of the screws before inserting them. Let the caulk dry, then install the new fixture on the mounting plate.

Removing & Replacing Broken Wall Tiles

1 Carefully scrape away the grout from the surrounding joints, using a utility knife or an awl. Break the damaged tile into small pieces, using a hammer and chisel. Remove the broken pieces, then scrape away debris or old adhesive from the open area.

2 If the tile to be replaced is a cut tile, cut a new one to match (see pages 98 to 103). Test-fit the new tile and make sure it sits flush with the field. Spread adhesive on the back of the replacement tile and place it in the hole, twisting it slightly. Use masking tape to hold the tile in place for 24 hours so the adhesive can dry.

3 Remove the tape, then apply premixed grout, using a sponge or grout float. Let the grout set slightly, then tool it with a rounded object such as a toothbrush handle. Wipe away excess grout with a damp cloth.

4 Let the grout dry for an hour, then polish the tile with a clean, dry cloth.

Maintaining Floor Tile

Tile floors are extremely durable, but they do require periodic maintenance. Accidents happen and although it takes quite an impact to break a floor tile, it is possible. Broken tile or failed grout can expose the underlayment to moisture which will destroy the floor in time.

Major cracks in grout joints indicate that movement of the floor has caused the adhesive layer beneath the tile to deteriorate. The adhesive layer must be replaced along with the grout in order to create a permanent repair.

Perhaps the biggest challenge with tile repair is matching the grout color. If you're regrouting an entire floor, just select the color that complements the tile; if you're replacing a tile, you have to blend the new grout with the old. A good tile dealer can help you get the best color match.

Any time you remove tile, check the underlayment.

If it's no longer smooth, solid, and level, repair or replace it before repairing the tile.

Protect unglazed tile from stains and water spots by periodically applying a coat of tile sealer. Keep dirt from getting trapped in grout lines by sealing them every year or two.

EVERYTHING YOU NEED

Tools: rotary tool, utility knife, or grout saw, hammer, cold chisel, eye protection, small screwdriver, putty knife, sponge, brush, stiff-bristled brush, bucket, rubber grout float.

Materials: grout, rubber gloves, grout float or sponge, soft cloth, grout sealer.

Regrouting a Ceramic Tile Floor

1 Completely remove the old grout, using a rotary tool, utility knife (and several blades), or a grout saw. Spread the new grout over the tiles, using a rubber grout float. Force grout into the joints, holding the float almost flat, then drag the float across the joints diagonally, tilting the face at a 45° angle.

2 Remove excess grout by making a second pass with the float. Work diagonally across the joint lines, and tilt the float at a steep angle to the tile faces.

3 Let the grout set for 10 to 15 minutes, then wipe away excess with a damp sponge, rinsing frequently. Fill in low spots by applying and smoothing extra grout with your finger. Let the grout dry for about an hour, then polish the tile faces with a dry cloth to remove the powdery residue. Seal the grout after it cures completely.

Replacing a Floor Tile

1 Remove the grout from around the damaged tile, using a rotary tool, utility knife (and several blades), or a grout saw. Then, carefully break apart the tile, using a cold chisel and hammer.

2 Scrape away the old adhesive with a putty knife. Make sure the base surface is smooth and flat.

3 Use a notched trowel to cover the entire back of the replacement tile with an even layer of thin-set mortar.

4 Set the tile in place, and press down firmly to create a good bond. If necessary, use a carpet-covered 2 × 4 and a rubber mallet to tap the tile flush with the neighboring tiles.

5 Use a small screwdriver to remove excess mortar that has oozed into the grout joints, then wipe up any mortar from the tile surface. When the mortar has dried completely, grout around the tile (page 240).

Maintaining Grout

Like the tile on your bathroom or kitchen walls, floor tile must be watertight. All the grout lines must be solid and full, and every tile must be free of cracks or chips. Neglecting problems can result in damage to the underlayment and subfloor, and possibly to the entire tile job.

Perhaps the greatest challenge with tile repair is matching the grout color. If you're regrouting an entire floor, just select a color that complements the tile; if you're replacing a tile, you have to blend the new grout with the old. A good tile dealer can help you get the best color match.

Apply grout sealer to grout joints every 1 to 2 years to protect against water, wear, and stains. Use a sponge brush to spread the sealer and keep it off the tiles. Allow new grout to cure fully before sealing it.

Glossary

American National Standards Institute (ANSI): A standards-making organization that rates tile for water permeability.

Art tiles: Hand-finished tiles with designs, pictures or patterns. Art tiles are often used to accent a large tile layout.

Back buttering: Spreading mortar on the back of a tile before pressing it onto the substrate.

Baseboard tile: Baseboard-shaped tiles used to replace wood baseboards.

Bullnose trim tile: Tile with one rounded edge that is meant to be left exposed.

Cement body tile: Tile made from concrete poured into forms.

Coefficient of friction: The measure of a tile's slip resistance. Tiles with high numbers are more slip resistant.

Decorative: Tile with designs, pictures, or relief. Decorative tiles are generally used as accents in a field of solid-color tiles.

Dry fit: Installing tile without mortar in order to test the layout.

Expansion joint: An expansion joint is a joint in a tile layout filled with a flexible material like caulk instead of grout. The expansion joint allows the tile to shift without cracking.

Field tiles: The main tile in a tile design. As opposed to trim or accent tiles.

Floor tile: Any type of tile designated for use on floors. It can generally also be used for walls or countertops.

Floor-warming systems: A system of heating elements installed directly under the floor material. Floor-warming systems are intended to provide supplemental radiant heat for a room.

Glass tile: Tile made of translucent glass. Glass tile is often used as accent tile.

Glazed ceramic: Tile made from refined clay that has been coated with a glaze and then fired in a kiln.

Grade: Ratings applied to some tile indicating the quality and consistency of manufacturing. Grade 1 tile is standard, suitable for most applications; grade 2 may have minor glaze and size imperfections; grade 3 tile is thin and suitable only for wall or decorative applications.

Grout: A dry powder, usually cement based, that is mixed with water and pressed into the joints between tiles. Grout also comes with latex or acrylic added for greater adhesion and impermeability.

Impervious: Tile that absorbs less than .5% of its weight in water.

Isolation membrane: Isolation membrane is a flexible material installed in sheets or troweled onto an unstable or damaged base floor, subfloor, or wall before installing tile. The isolation membrane prevents shifts in the base from damaging the tile above.

Joists: The framing members that support the floor.

Kiln: A high-temperature oven used to harden clay tile.

Liners: Narrow tiles used for adding contrasting lines to tile layouts.

Listello: A border tile, usually with a raised design. Also called listel.

Mastic or organic mastic: A type of glue for installing tile. It comes premixed and cures as it dries. It is convenient for wall tiles smaller than 6 × 6, but it is not suitable for floors.

Metal tile: Tile made of iron, stainless steel, copper, or brass. Metal tile is often used as accent tile.

Mortar or thin-set mortar: A mixture of portland cement and sand and occasionally a latex or acrylic additive to improve adhesion.

Mosaic tile: Small colored tiles used to make patterns or pictures on walls and floors.

Natural stone tile: Tile cut from marble, slate, granite, or other natural stone.

Non-vitreous: Very permeable tile. Non-vitreous tile absorbs more than 7% of its total weight in water. Not suitable for outdoor installations.

Porcelain Enamel Institute (PEI): A tile industry group that issues ratings on tile's resistance to wear.

Porcelain tile: Tile made from refined white clay fired at high temperatures. Porcelain is usually dyed rather than glazed, and thus its color runs the tile's full thickness.

Quarry tile: Tile formed to look like quarried stone.

Reference lines: Lines marked on the substrate to guide the placement of the first row of tile.

Saltillo: Terra-cotta tile from Mexico. Saltillos have a distinctly rustic appearance.

Sealants: Sealants protect non- and semi-vitreous tile from stains and from water damage. Sealants are also important for protecting grout.

Self-spacing tile: Tile with attached tabs for maintaining even spacing.

Semi-vitreous: Moderately permeable tile. Absorbs 3-7% of its total weight in water. Not suitable for outdoor installations.

Spacers: Plastic lugs meant to be inserted between tiles to help maintain uniform spacing during installation.

Story stick: A length of 1 x 2 lumbar marked with the tile spacing for a specific layout.

Subfloor: The surface, usually made of plywood, attached to the floor joists.

Substrates or underlayment: A surface installed on top of an existing floor, subfloor, or wall. The substrate creates a suitable surface for installing tile. Substrate materials include cementboard, plywood, cork, backerboard, greenboard, or water-proofing membrane.

Terra-cotta tile: Tile made from unrefined clay. Terra-cotta is fired at low temperature. Its color varies greatly depending on where the source of the clay.

Trim tile: Tile with a finished edge for completing wall tile layouts.

V-cap tiles: V- or L-shaped tile for finishing the exposed edges of countertops.

Vitreous: Slightly permeable tile. Absorbs .5-3% of its total weight in water.

Wall tile: Tile intended for use on walls. It is generally thinner than floor tile and should not be used on floors or countertops.

Water absorption or permeability: The measure of the amount of water that will penetrate a tile when it is wet. Measurement ranges from non-vitreous to semi-vitreous to vitreous to impervious.

Waterproofing membrane: A flexible, water-proof material installed in sheets or brushed on to protect the subfloor from water damage.

Contributors

A special thanks for contributing samples and allowing us open access to their facility:

Rubble Tile
6001 Culligan Way
Minnetonka, MN 55345
952-938-2599
www.rubbletile.com

Buddy Rhodes Studio
877-706-5303
www.buddyrhodes.com
photo on p. 141 (right) by photographer, Ken Gutmaker; kitchen design, www.johnnygrey.com

Country Floors, Inc.
Sicis
800-311-9995
www.countryfloors.com
Since 1964, Preserving great American & European tile-making traditions. Country Floors, Inc. has branch showrooms in the following locations:
Los Angeles, CA; San Francisco, CA; New York, N.Y.; Greenwich, CT; Dania Beach, FL; Montreal, Quebec; Toronto, Ontario

Ceramic Tiles of Italy
212-980-1500
www.italytile.com.
The following photos feature tiles from these Italian companies:
p. 7 (bottom) Provenza, www.ceramicheprovenza.com; p. 8 (top) Ragno, www.ragno.it; p. 8 (bottom) Provenza, wwwceramicheprovenza.com; p. 20 Rasseno, www.bellanoceramictile.com; p. 22 Lux, www.lux.riwal.it; p. 26 (right) Alfa, www.alfa.riwal.it; p. 27 (bottom right) Saime, www.saime.riwal.it; p. 29 (bottom right) Piemme, www.ceramichepienne.it; p. 31 Marca Corona, www.marcacorona.it; p. 109 (top left) Italgraniti, www.italgraniti.it; p. 109 (top right) Sire, www.klinkersire.com; p. 110 (top right) Panaria, www.panaria.it; p .112 Edilgres Sirio, www.edilgres-sirio.it; p. 113 (top right) Century, www.monocibec.it; p. 114 (bottom) Ker-Ex, www.kerex.it; p. 145 (top right) Brennero, www.brennero.com; p. 145 (bottom) Elios, www.eliosceramica.com; p. 146 (bottom) Novabell, www.novabell.it; p. 147 Grazia, www.ceramiche-grazia.it; p. 148 Ricchetti, www.ricchetti.it; p. 151 Imola, www.imolaceramica.it; p. 153 (top) Magica, www.cermagica.it; p. 153 (center) RioKerfin, www.alfa.riwal.it; p. 153 (bottom) Francesco De Maio, www.francescodemaio.it; p. 154 Cemar, www.cemarint.com; p. 171 (top left) Marmo, www.marmo.it; p. 184 (top right) Ker-Av, www.kerav.co; p. 188 (top left) La Tavolozza Vietrese, www.tavolozzavietrese.it

Crossville Porcelain Stone
P.O. Box 1168
Crossville, TN 38557
931-484-2110
www.crossvilleceramics.com

Daltile
800-933-TILE
www.daltile.com

d'facto Art, Inc.
952-906-1003
www.dfactoart.com

Dock 6 Pottery
Kerry Brooks
612-379-2110
www.dock6pottery.com

EuroTile Featuring Villi® Glas
239-275-8033
www.villiglass.com

Fireclay Tile, Inc.
408-275-1182
www.fireclaytile.com

Hi-Ho Industries, Inc.
Mosaic-Tile Arts
St. Paul, MN
651-649-0992

IKEA Home Furnishings
496 W. Germantown Pike
Plymouth Meeting, PA 19462
800-434-4532

Broken china tiles and other mosaic supplies as shown on p. 202 available from:
KPTiles
Kristen Phillips
248-853-0418
www.kptiles.com

Meredith Collection
330-484-4887
www.meredithtile.com

Montana Tile & Stone Co.
58 Peregrine Way
Bozeman, MT 59718
406-587-6114
www.montanatile.com

Oceanside Glasstile™
760-929-5882
www.glasstile.com
Photo on p. 24 (right) by Christopher Ray Photography

Tile Creator™
760-788-1288
www.tilecreator.com

Walker & Zanger, Inc.
13190 Telfair Avenue
Sylmar, CA 91342
818-504-0235
www.walkerzanger.com

Photographers

Beateworks, Inc.
Los Angeles, CA
www.beateworks.com
p.184 (bottom) ©Baerdemaeker/Inside/Beateworks.com; p. 185 ©Henry Cabala/Beateworks.com; p.151 (top left) ©Caillaut/Inside/Beateworks.com; p. 9 ©Chabaneix/Inside/Beateworks.com; p. 146 (top right) ©Claessens/Inside/Beateworks.com; p. 144 ©Christopher Covey/Beateworks.com; p. 206 (top right) ©Duronsoy/Inside/Beateworks.com; p. 184 (top left) ©Galeron/Inside/Beateworks.com; p. 206 (top left) ©Douglas Hill/Beateworks.com; p. 17 ©Palisse/Inside/Beateworks.com; pp. 29 (left), 80, 146 (top left),152 (top), 173, 175, 187 (top), 204, 206 (bottom), 207, 209 (top left) ©Tim Street-Porter/Beateworks.com; p. 6 ©Touillon/Inside/Beateworks.com; p. 115 ©Vasseur/Inside/Beateworks.com; p. 21 ©Van Robaeys/Inside/Beateworks.com

Index Stock Imagery, Inc.
New York, NY
www.indexstock.com
p. 213 (top) ©Index Stock Imagery Inc./Shubroto Chattopadhyay; pp. 182-3, 213 (bottom) ©Index Stock Imagery, Inc./Kindra Clineff; p. 210 (top) ©Index Stock Imagery, Inc./Diaphor Agency; p. 212 ©Index Stock Imagery Inc./FotoKIA; p. 210 (bottom) ©Index Stock Imagery Inc./Stephen Saks; p. 211 ©Index Stock Imagery Inc./Lousi Yanucci

David Livingston Photography
Mill Valley, CA
©www.davidduncanlivingston.com: p. 186

Mosaic mural image on p. 200 is based on the painting *Calabash Girls* by Tilly Willis, 1991 (oil on canvas)

Resources

American Society of Interior Designers
202-546-3480
www.asid.org

Center for Universal Design NC State University
919-515-3082
www.design.ncsu.edu/cud

Construction Materials Recycling Association
630-548-4510
www.cdrecycling.org

Energy & Environmental Building Association
952-881-1098
www.eeba.org

International Residential Code Book
International Conference of Building Officials
800-284-4406
www.icbo.com

National Kitchen & Bath Association (NKBA)
800-843-6522
www.nkba.org

The Tile Council of America, Inc.
864-646-8453
www.tileusa.com

U.S. Environmental Protection Agency—
Indoor Air Quality
www.epa.gov/iedweb00/pubs/insidest.html

Conversion Charts

Drill Bit Guide

Twist Bit   **Self-piloting**   **Spade Bit**   **Adjustable Counterbore**   **Hole Saw**

 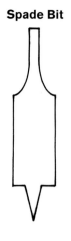 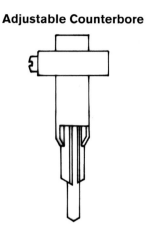 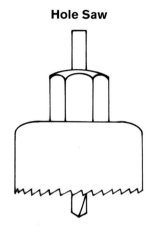

Counterbore, Shank & Pilot Hole Diameters

Screw Size	Counterbore Diameter for Screw Head	Clearance Hole for Screw Shank	Pilot Hole Diameter	
			Hard Wood	**Soft Wood**
#1	.146 (9/64)	5/64	3/64	1/32
#2	1/4	3/32	3/64	1/32
#3	1/4	7/64	1/16	3/64
#4	1/4	1/8	1/16	3/64
#5	1/4	1/8	5/64	1/16
#6	5/16	9/64	3/32	5/64
#7	5/16	5/32	3/32	5/64
#8	3/8	11/64	1/8	3/32
#9	3/8	11/64	1/8	3/32
#10	3/8	3/16	1/8	7/64
#11	1/2	3/16	5/32	9/64
#12	1/2	7/32	9/64	1/8

Abrasive Paper Grits - (Aluminum Oxide)

Very Coarse	Coarse	Medium	Fine	Very Fine
12 - 36	40 - 60	80 - 120	150 - 180	220 - 600

Saw Blades

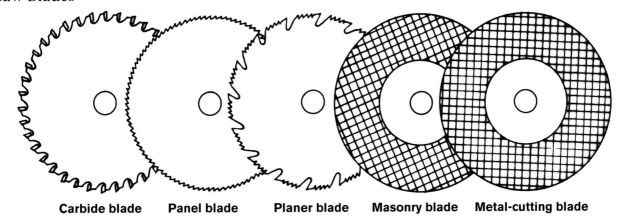

Carbide blade   **Panel blade**   **Planer blade**   **Masonry blade**   **Metal-cutting blade**

Adhesives

Type	Characteristics	Uses
White glue	**Strength:** moderate; rigid bond **Drying time:** several hours **Resistance to heat:** poor **Resistance to moisture:** poor **Hazards:** none **Cleanup/solvent:** soap and water	**Porous surfaces:** Wood (indoors) Paper Cloth
Yellow glue (carpenter's glue)	**Strength:** moderate to good; rigid bond **Drying time:** several hours; faster than white glue **Resistance to heat:** moderate **Resistance to moisture:** moderate **Hazards:** none **Cleanup/solvent:** soap and water	**Porous surfaces:** Wood (indoors) Paper Cloth
Two-part epoxy	**Strength:** excellent; strongest of all adhesives **Drying time:** varies, depending on manufacturer **Resistance to heat:** excellent **Resistance to moisture:** excellent **Hazards:** fumes are toxic and flammable **Cleanup/solvent:** acetone will dissolve some types	**Smooth & porous surfaces:** Wood (indoors & outdoors) Metal Masonry Glass Fiberglass
Hot glue	**Strength:** depends on type **Drying time:** less than 60 seconds **Resistance to heat:** fair **Resistance to moisture:** good **Hazards:** hot glue can cause burns **Cleanup/solvent:** heat will loosen bond	**Smooth & porous surfaces:** Glass Plastics Wood
Cyanoacrylate (instant glue)	**Strength:** excellent, but with little flexibility **Drying time:** a few seconds **Resistance to heat:** excellent **Resistance to moisture:** excellent **Hazards:** can bond skin instantly; toxic, flammable **Cleanup/solvent:** acetone	**Smooth surfaces:** Glass Ceramics Plastics Metal
Construction adhesive	**Strength:** good to excellent; very durable **Drying time:** 24 hours **Resistance to heat:** good **Resistance to moisture:** excellent **Hazards:** may irritate skin and eyes **Cleanup/solvent:** soap and water (while still wet)	**Porous surfaces:** Framing lumber Plywood and paneling Wallboard Foam panels Masonry
Water-base contact cement	**Strength:** good **Drying time:** bonds instantly; dries fully in 30 minutes **Resistance to heat:** excellent **Resistance to moisture:** good **Hazards:** may irritate skin and eyes **Cleanup/solvent:** soap and water (while still wet)	**Porous surfaces:** Plastic laminates Plywood Flooring Cloth
Silicone sealant (caulk)	**Strength:** fair to good; very flexible bond **Drying time:** 24 hours **Resistance to heat:** good **Resistance to moisture:** excellent **Hazards:** may irritate skin and eyes **Cleanup/solvent:** acetone	**Smooth & porous surfaces:** Wood Ceramics Fiberglass Plastics Glass

Index

(continued next page)

(continued next page)

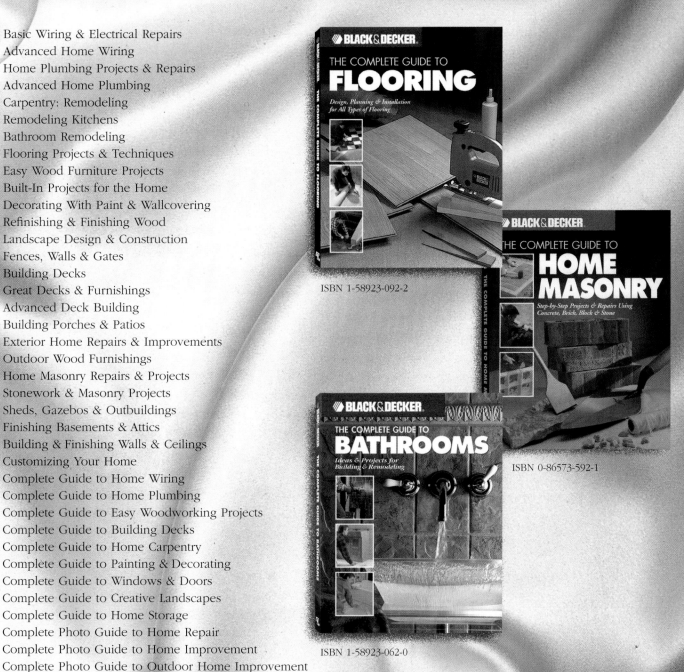